CONTENTS

Ships in Focus Publications

Correspondence and editorial:
Roy Fenton
18 Durrington Avenue
London SW20 8NT
020 8879 3527
rfenton@rfenton.demon.co.uk

Orders and photographic:
John & Marion Clarkson
18 Franklands, Longton
Preston PR4 5PD
01772 612855
shipsinfocus@btinternet.com

Printed by Amadeus Press Ltd., Cleckheaton,
Yorkshire.
Designed by Hugh Smallwood, John Clarkson
and Roy Fenton.
SHIPS IN FOCUS RECORD
ISBN 978-1-901703-88-7

SUBSCRIPTION RATES FOR RECORD

Readers can start their subscription with
any issue, and are welcome to backdate it to
receive previous issues.

	3 issues	4 issues
UK	£24	£31
Europe (airmail)	£26	£34
Rest of the world (surface mail)	£26	£34
Rest of the world (airmail)	£31	£41

SHIPS IN FOCU
March

When we set out to compose this editorial in January 2009 ...
to suggest areas that potential authors might like to research for future issues.
However, writers have been particularly busy over the Christmas period, and
we have had a plethora of submissions and firm promises of articles. We are in
the happy position of being able to plan our issues at least one year ahead, but
needless to say we will not turn away any promising material. However, what we
are lacking is a 'Photographer in Focus' feature, in which we showcase the work
of a capable ship photographer and give brief details of his life and work. Offers
are invited although, to avoid embarrassing the living, we do insist that the subject
is dead.

The Ships in Focus policy of crediting photographs has been evolving,
and we now aim to mention both the person who made the original exposure and
the name of whoever provided us with the image - whether as print, negative or
high-resolution scan. The second name given in the credits recognises that the
collector has acquired the photograph, looked after it, and has been kind enough to
retrieve it and loan it to us. Whenever possible we source photographs ourselves,
but only by using other collections can we give the depth of coverage we aim for
in this journal and in our books.

Without such often 'private' collections, our choice of illustration would
be limited. Sadly, the cost of obtaining and using photographs from certain
museums and other 'public' collections often puts them beyond consideration.
A museum is entitled to expect some return on its material (although often it
was donated for free), but to charge so much as to prohibit reproduction in a
specialised journal like ours seems counter productive. Surely, a modest return
is better than none at all, and our using the photograph does mean interested
individuals can see it, which was surely the reason the image was donated to or
acquired by the museum.

There are, of course, honourable exceptions; institutions who allow
reasonable reproduction, as readers can see from the credits under photographs,
and institutions which we thank heartily. One credit readers will not see is that for
the Merseyside Maritime Museum which has put some of its negative collections
into cold storage, quite literally. This will certainly keep them safe, as they are
now completely inaccessible. One would like to know the reasoning behind this,
as burying them in a freezer is not a zero-cost exercise, and precludes their use.
In addition, the majority of film and glass plate negatives seem not to deteriorate
in use: some of the negatives regularly used to obtain images for 'Record' will be
getting on for 100 years old and are in perfect condition.

We end this short homily by repeating our request, first made some years
ago, that anyone disposing of a collection of prints or negatives chiefly comprised
of ships built before about 1970 should consider Ships in Focus as a possible
recipient. As we have done with collections already acquired, we will use them
in our publications for the enjoyment of others and, if required, will respect the
previous owner's wishes for their ultimate disposal.

John Clarkson
Roy Fenton

March 2009

The Liberty *Samboston* was photographed in Ellerman colours at Swansea on
or about 15th June 1947. A detailed feature on the Liberties loaned to the UK
begins on page 103. *[National Maritime Museum N58716]*

Black Prince of 1955 (above) and
Northumbrian Prince of 1956 (below),
the latter outward bound on the River
Mersey in 1957. This pairing serves
to show the similarities of the four- and
three-hatch design Mediterranean
traders of Prince Line, especially the
treatment of the superstructure. *Black
Prince*, however, has significantly
enhanced cargo equipment in the
form of kingposts and derricks ahead
and abaft of the superstructure. *[W.T.
Hubbard/Roy Fenton collection;
Stewart Bale 561143-2/Author's
collection]*

Fleet in Focus

PRINCE LINE MEDITERRANEAN SHIPS POST-1945: Part 2

George Swaine

Pre-war ships replaced

By now, the pre-war ships were worked out and were retired from the trade as further replacements were delivered from Burntisland. The *Palestinian Prince* ended up trading under the auspices of Furness Withy Montreal, supplying Goose Bay in Labrador with general cargo, foodstuffs and machinery in the open season with a backhaul of pulpwood logs for the Newfoundland paper mills at Cornerbrook and Stephenville. The next batch of four-hatch ships - *Beechmore/English Prince* (2) (yard number 353), *Black Prince* (4) (yard number 354) and *Pinemore/African Prince* (5) (yard number 355) - were all delivered within a year during 1954 and 1955. Again, they were slightly larger with a deadweight increased to 4,900 tons, increased refrigerated capacity and a more efficient Hawthorn, Leslie-built Doxford diesel giving a service speed of 13.5 knots. They were perhaps the most aesthetically satisfying of this series, with a raked funnel, unobtrusive mushroom ventilators and lifeboats placed at the after end of the boat deck, slung from Schat gravity davits. They were almost immediately followed by two smaller three-hatch versions, the *Norman Prince* (5) (yard number 374) and *Northumbrian Prince* (yard number 375) delivered in 1956. Apart from the raked funnel, differing lifeboat disposition and other details referred to above, these latter ships could be instantly differentiated from the *Maltese Prince* and *Cyprian Prince* by having the main mast placed aft of number 3 hatch.

Shortly after completion *Beechmore* and *Pinemore* were adapted for trading to the Great Lakes as far as Chicago through the newly-opened St. Lawrence Seaway during the open water season. The alterations, required for transiting the many unmanned automatic locks, took the form of fitting Colborne leads, 'whisker' booms and half-round permanent steel fender bars amidships as well as a stern anchor and a massive state-of-the-art Marconi installation on the bridge. This apparatus, at least the size of a large wardrobe, was designed to facilitate short-range communication during Seaway transits, but was extremely temperamental, once being described by an exasperated mate as 'a complete horse's arse'. Occasionally the same two ships were employed on the North Atlantic Furness Warren Line service between Liverpool, Newfoundland, the Maritimes and Boston. They would then switch to the Johnson Warren Line Mediterranean and Black Sea service or go on the Prince Line berth. These examples demonstrate how difficult it is to pick out the separate lines and services from the intricacies of one of the most complex of the major shipping groups.

The last ship in this series of 11 vessels, all built to the same general pattern by Burntisland, was the *Lancastrian Prince* (5) (yard number 395) delivered in 1960. Deadweight had increased to 5,650 tons and service speed to 14 knots. As mentioned earlier, the capstan and winches were all electrically driven with an improved form

of automatic topping lift. Topmasts were eliminated with a combined signal and radar mast just forward of the funnel.

A typical voyage

The Mediterranean trade settled down until the late 1960s with the three-hatch ships based in Manchester and the four-hatch vessels sailing out of London, exporting manufactured goods from the UK and Continent and importing agricultural produce. Occasionally large contracts would dominate or at least influence the trading pattern. One typical example was the export of many hundred Centurion Mark V tanks, each weighing 50 tons, to Israel. In attempting to recreate a typical voyage of the time, I have looked at a number of freight reports, cadets' journals and company correspondence of the time and, in what follows, all of the incidents described actually took place. It should be remembered that Prince Line, as was the case with other lines, paid considerable attention to the complex matter of cargo stowage and care in those pre-container days. One of the earlier generation of Prince Line superintendents, Captain R.E. Thomas, was the author of the standard textbook on stowage known throughout the mercantile marine as 'Thomas's Stowage.' The early editions of this book advised anxious officers on the preferred stowage of such esoteric commodities as 'dogs' droppings from the Persian Gulf' (on deck, thankfully) and how to qualify a boat note in order to produce a valid mate's receipt – 'three elephants delivered on board, one in dispute, if on board to be delivered.' Captain Thomas also invented a locking hatch bar and, perhaps more significantly, the T&B roller hatch beam with which all Furness ships were fitted prior to the advent of MacGregor automatic steel hatch covers. Another widely used cargo manual by Taylor and Trim recommended Prince Line documentation as examples of good practice.

Early in February 1958 a two-year-old Prince boat lay alongside the load berth in Salford, loading an outward cargo of pipes, tractors, trucks, harvesters, cars (Austin Cambridge), naval stores for Malta, ammunition for Cyprus and 1,000 cases of whisky. A port relief crew of chief, second and third officers were kept busy sorting out cargo stowages with stevedores, supervising repairs and surveys. One deck apprentice – known as a cadet in this company – also stood by whilst the other two cadets were on leave. Having drawn the short straw, the duty cadet was on call for any task decided by the mate and this could encompass anything and everything. After a 05.30 call by the night watchman, cargo lights, other lights, flags, removal of hatch locking bars had to be attended to, all in time for commencement of cargo work. If the night watchman had forgotten to light the galley stove ready for the cooks to start work, this job fell to the cadet and proved to be an exciting interlude. The oil sprayers had to be turned on whilst a sheet of newspaper was lit and tossed in. As may be imagined, a certain degree of dexterity and timing were essential to avoid undesirable consequences, namely the cook appearing after a failure and directing a string of epithets towards the ancestry of the cadet. No health and safety guidelines were available nor any counselling to ease any possible resulting distress to the lad. The cadet then shifted into uniform for breakfast and immediately afterwards back into working gear. He would sound all fresh water, ballast and oil tanks and complete the sounding book, reporting to the chief officer for orders to fill tanks or adjust ballast tanks as necessary. It may be that he would then have to scrub out the cargo chill chambers and prepare them to receive cargo, following which he was ordered to shift into uniform again and stand by to welcome superintendents, shippers or freight managers to a special luncheon. No seamen were on board and if there were specific tasks such as breaking out the heavy-lift derrick or shifting the ship along the quay, the Furness gang of shore riggers, shared with the bigger *Pacific* ships (see Ships in Focus 'Record' 14 and 15) which also used Manchester, would be called upon. Similarly, engineers standing by were perhaps one senior and two juniors on day work. With only one of the Sunderland Forge generators throbbing away to supply power and the main boiler supplying steam for this plus any cargo winches that may be required, port manning could be reduced to a minimum.

Depending on cargo requirements, anywhere between ten and fifteen days could be spent in Manchester. As cargo work drew to a completion, a quickening pace was noticeable. The sailing officers would join and the crew signed on. Whilst their contemporaries in other Furness companies would join an outward-bound cargo liner with 60 or 70 crew with a voyage to South America, West Coast USA or Australasia of three or more months in prospect, these small ships carried a crew of 36 and anticipated a typical trip of around six weeks. Together with 12 passengers, this meant 48 people on a ship which today might be manned by one seventh of that number.

After transiting the Manchester Ship Canal, the ship proceeded to Barry in South Wales, where 21 Saladin armoured cars were loaded for the British Army in Libya. She then sailed along the Welsh coast as far as Milford Haven, anchoring off to await the arrival from Glasgow of an ICI coaster, the *Lady Anstruther* (547/1946). Before leaving Manchester, special magazines had been constructed in the 'tween decks to carry 5,000 cases of seismic gelignite for the oil exploration teams in the Libyan desert. On completion of cargo work everything was secured and course set for the first foreign port, Ceuta, where bunkers were normally taken for the round voyage. During that first night, the weather gradually worsened to force 8 and when the cadets were called for the 4-to-8 watch the following morning they were informed that the steering engine had broken down and that the ship was seeking a port of refuge. Emergency hand tackles kept in the steering flat were rigged and hand steering employed. Helm orders

were relayed from the emergency compass on the after accommodation by using a hose pipe and the master on the bridge kept in touch with the after gang using the docking telephone. It was all very primitive by today's standards, but it worked. Arriving off Falmouth, and on learning of the dangerous nature of her cargo, the ship was warned to stay some distance outside the channel between St Mawes and Pendennis Castles. Although the restriction slowed repairs, these were completed by the evening of the following day and the voyage resumed.

Southbound, the weather worsened until a full storm was in progress. In all, three days were spent hove to and considerable, if superficial damage, was inflicted. By the time of arrival at Ceuta less than a day's fuel was left on board. None of this stopped the relentless round of maintenance of cargo gear, with a complete wash down and holystoning of the boat and passenger decks early each morning at sea as the weather improved.

To take advantage of the favourable easterly current, the ships would keep close to the North African shore when outbound. In those days, this meant that a French Air Force plane would invariably buzz the vessel numerous times during her progress along the Algerian coast, this being a precaution against gun running during the savage war waged prior to independence. The first cargo port on this voyage was Tunis, reached by proceeding up a rather smelly canal from La Goulette, near the ruins of Carthage. After the cargo was discharged, two thoroughbred horses were taken on board and tethered by number 2 hatch for overnight carriage to Malta.

Inevitably the cadets were ordered to look after the animals and the senior cadet so arranged the watch duties that the junior cadet would not be 'first or second wheel' but the 'farmer'. Apart from two hours on lookout, this meant that he had the job of feeding and tending the horses both on and off watch and ensuring all was in order for the ship's arrival at Malta the following morning. The ship duly arrived off Valetta early the next day and proceeded up the magnificent Grand Harbour to her berth at the Marsa. Numerous warships, including HMS *Ark Royal, Eagle* and *Tiger* plus some US vessels, were moored in the harbour.

Norman Prince (5) moored stern on at Marsa Creek, Malta, about 1958 alongside *Balzac* of Fred. Olsen. The port lifeboat is being exercised. *[A.J.B. Davidson/ Author's collection]*

As the ship passed, more and more sailors rushed to the side of the flight decks and started cheering and pointing. The master was puzzled for a moment; what could be the matter? Looking over the bridge front to number 2 hatch solved the conundrum. There the stallion and mare were heavily engaged in an activity which horses have performed at regular intervals since the dawn of time and which in any case, as the rueful junior cadet pointed out to his unsympathetic comrades in the halfdeck after yet another verbal roasting, was the specific reason the blessed nags had been sent to Malta.

Three days later in Tripoli, excitement of a different nature occurred when stevedores discharging the ICI seismic gelignite were discovered nonchalantly cooking their midday meal over an open fire in the depths of the magazine. When calling at Alexandria, it was customary for Furness (Egypt) - one of the innumerable group companies all over the globe - to arrange for hundreds of labourers to descend on the ship to scale and coat the hull in red lead. The deafening racket continued night and day so that all on board were glad to depart. The pace of work quickened around Eastern Mediterranean ports. For example, Beirut (always a popular port), Tripoli (Lebanon), Lattakia, Morphou Bay, Limassol (twice), Zyyi and Famagusta were visited during this voyage within the space of ten days. One interesting if little known fact is that all Prince Line masters on their first call in command to Beirut were presented with an impressively large gold signet ring engraved with the Cedar of Lebanon. Some captains wore it all the time; some only put it on each time the Beirut pilot boarded. The pilot service was in the gift of one family - the Baltigis - for many years, and they and Prince Line's long-standing agents in Lebanon had organised the ring presentations. I suppose it was not dissimilar to the gold-topped canes presented to the first master to transit the St Lawrence or reach Churchill in Hudson Bay in the open water season, but not as well known.

The hectic schedule necessitated anchoring, derricks and hatches all being worked and secured constantly, sometimes for a cargo of, say, 40 tons of wine in casks being loaded from barges at an open roadstead. The final port of Famagusta was something of a respite, perhaps five or six days being taken to discharge Army ammunition and stores and load a full cargo of citrus. Despite the tensions of the Eoka situation, crews always looked forward to Famagusta for the rest from watch keeping afforded during the stay. Swimming was possible during 'smokoes' on the nearby deserted beaches. Films were organised by the resident Royal Navy minesweeper squadron engaged on terrorist patrol and were viewed on a screen hung from the Venetian ramparts surrounding the old city captured by the Turks in 1580. Later,

Lancastrian Prince (5) before commencing loading citrus at Famagusta, Cyprus about 1961 with *Ausonia* (11,879/1957) of Adriatica Line astern of her. *[Furness Withy/Author's collection]*

brandy sours beckoned at the Harbour Bar in Varosha, the new quarter, known as Greek Town. Not a tourist in sight.

Full opportunity was taken in 'Fama – G' to paint ship from the quay, the painting punt and from stages so that, on final departure homeward bound, the ship looked immaculate with the chief officer praying for fair weather in order that the decks could be painted on passage. As well as a good cargo turn out, his reputation with the unforgiving gods in the Marine Superintendents' Department depended to a certain extent on arriving in the UK with a pristine ship with all necessary work and maintenance performed. All, alas, was to descend into chaos as soon as stevedores swarmed on board in London, Liverpool or Manchester.

On passage, besides keeping the 12-to-4 watch and being responsible for the navigation, the second officer would be engaged in elaborate wage calculations without the assistance of computers or calculators to complete the large and complex portage bill. The crew were paid off in cash on board so a radio message had to be sent to the Furness office requesting that an appropriate amount of cash be delivered on board by the port agent on arrival to be divided into pay packets quickly and accurately. Particular nightmares were fog delays or missing the tide so that further last minute calculations became necessary. To avoid this problem on the London bound ships, experienced navigators had a trick up their sleeves, by attempting to ensure that arrival at the Dover Straits was a little in advance of high water. This would mean the sea and Thames river pilotages and docking were on the flood, the ship having 'changed buses' in a tidal sense to take advantage of the southerly North Sea flood stream. Larger Furness ships would take an accountant on board for the coastal passage to assist in this work, whilst other group companies may have carried pursers or writers. No such luck for those on the little Meddy boats.

Malvern Prince of 1970 introduced a new element to the Prince Line naming scheme, ranges of hills in southern England. *Malvern Prince* was photographed on the New Waterway in June 1971. *[J. and M. Clarkson collection]*

The final Mediterranean ships

As the sixties progressed, the withdrawal of Britain from military bases, increasing stevedoring, crew and other running costs, the advent of national shipping lines, tourist travel by air, road haulage and ro-ros, all conspired to reduce the profitability of the trade. The radical effects of the bulk and container revolution which would change the technical, legal and commercial aspects of sea transport out of all recognition were not yet widely felt, but were discernible by those in management whose task was to see and plan ahead. By 1969 most of the earlier post-war buildings had been sold out of service and within the next two years the remainder would follow, the last, *Lancastrian Prince*, having served for a comparatively brief 11 years.

The trade was serviced by smaller chartered in tonnage, mainly German controlled. To some extent this need was reduced in 1970 by entry into service of the final series of conventional ships to be ordered by Prince Line. By now the political complexity of choosing suitable names had defeated the owners, who called the new ships after English hills – *Malvern Prince* (Grangemouth Dockyard, 1970), with *Chiltern Prince*, *Mendip/Cheviot Prince* (name altered in 1974) and *Cotswold Prince* all being completed by Clelands at Wallsend in 1970. They, too, maintained the Prince Line tradition of smartness but in truth were much smaller ships with two holds, no passengers and a significantly reduced crew. The ships had an English Electric nine-cylinder diesel of 2,400 BHP giving a service

When sold in 1971, *Black Prince* became *Maria B* under the Greek flag. Registered in the ownership of Intermar Services Co. S.A., Panama, owner was in fact G. Bobolas of Athens, whose initials can be discerned on her funnel. Her end came in March 1977 when she was abandoned after an engine room fire off West Africa whilst on passage from Las Palmas to Port Harcourt. *[Airfoto of Malacca/Ships in Focus collection]*

speed of 13 knots. Four 10-ton single swinging derricks of the Speedcrane type served the two holds.

A further not dissimilar vessel, the *Saxon Prince*, launched in Holland in 1971 as the *Cairntrader* for another group subsidiary, Cairn Line, and managed by yet another Furness company, Shaw Savill and Albion, joined the Prince Line at this time. Some of her sisters were sold to other British companies and chartered back.

In November 1970 the full effect of the rapidly escalating costs and reducing economic viability of conventional ships was to be felt by the Furness Group. On Friday 13th it was announced that 23 ships would be sold and that Furness Withy would no longer be an active ship owner, leaving the residual trades to be managed by subsidiaries, broadly divided into bulk and general cargo.

Most of the convolutions experienced by this complex organisation are beyond the scope of this article. The Prince Line traded through the 1970s in cooperation with another Furness company, Manchester Liners, who had turned their attention to the Middle East and had applied their container expertise to managing container terminals in Saudi Arabia. A small container ship, the *Pennine Prince*, was also completed in Holland in 1971 to work in conjunction with the conventional *Malvern Prince* class. She bore the distinction of having three different names whilst in service, being renamed *Sailor Prince* in 1972 and *Soldier Prince* five years later. This ship was the only two-funnelled vessel ever to carry the Prince Line colours, although an interesting historical note reveals that might not have been the case. In 1905, Sir James Knott ordered two sisters - passenger ships with two funnels - from the James Laing yard in Sunderland. These were provisionally named *Piedmontese Prince* and *Sardinian Prince*. By 1907 the Italian Government was insisting that the Italy to New York service, for which these ships were designed, should come under Italian control. Thus they were sold on the stocks and completed in 1907 as *Re d'Italia* and *Regina d'Italia* (both 6,149/1907) respectively. These were the first two vessels to be owned by Lloyd Sabaudo whose final ship before Mussolini's nationalisation of the Italian fleet was the famous *Conte Di Savoia* (48,502/1932).

The last two ships ever to be built for Prince Line were also container ships completed at the end of the decade, *Crown Prince* and *Royal Prince*, both by Swan Hunter and entering service in 1979.

Almost immediately the C.Y. Tung take-over of Furness Withy in 1980 followed by the enormous financial difficulties of this Hong Kong-based group saw the rapid withdrawal from services and sale of many Furness ships. Effectively, although the name lived on through another take-over by the German Oetker group in 1990, Prince had become defunct in all but name and their long-standing and notable presence in the Mediterranean trade relegated to the history books.

The cellular container ship *Royal Prince* of 1979 was the last ship delivered to Prince Line. *[Fotoflite incorporating Skyfotos 251527]*

The four-hatch *Beechmore* (3,596/1954) was completed for Johnston Warren Lines (upper). Only in 1965 was she transferred to Prince Line to become *English Prince* (2): note the addition of a badge to the bridge front and earlier modifications for trading to the Great Lakes including Colborne leads, fender bars and a stern anchor (middle). A fire in a cotton cargo at Charleston during December 1968 ended her Prince career, and she was sold unrepaired to Greek owners as *Mandraki* who put her back into service (bottom). There followed a string of renamings – to *Naftilos*, *Mariber* and *Mari* – and another fire, off Zadar, Yugoslavia in July 1978. This time there was no reprieve and she was scrapped at Split later that year. *[Roy Fenton collection; World Ship Society Ltd./ Author's collection; Airfoto of Malacca/J. and M. Clarkson collection]*

Second of her class of four-hatch ships, *Black Prince* (4) (3,597/1955) displays the slightly raked funnel design which considerably improved this group's appearance (top). She spent an uninterrupted 16 years under this name. *[Roy Fenton collection]*
Remarkably, all three of this class were to end their lives in flames. The third was completed as *Pinemore* (3,597/1955) for Johnston Warren (left, taken 16th September 1961), only becoming *African Prince* (6) in 1965 (bottom). Sold in 1971 she was renamed *Maldive Mail*, but survived just four years as this. In May 1975 her cargo caught fire whilst she was off the Indian coast and she was abandoned, to drift ashore, break in two and sink. *[C.L. Reynolds; Ships in Focus]*

Norman Prince (5) (2,709/1956) had a relatively short Prince Line career, sold to Greek owners in 1968 to take the first of five names, *Salamina*. She subsequently became *Dalmarin*, *Dodo*, *George SI* and *P. Dolores*. Fire was to claim her, too: in October 1975 an engine room blaze led to her being abandoned in the Mediterranean, after which she drifted ashore on the Moroccan coast. *[J. Campbell Harper Ltd./Author's collection]*

Northumbrian Prince (2,709/1956) at London in 1958. It is reported that she was intended to be named *Novocastrian Prince*. After her sale in 1968 she carried five further names – *Eleftheotria*, *Rodania*, *Omar*, *Suraj* and *Karari* – before being demolished at Gadani Beach in 1985. *[J. and M. Clarkson collection]*

Lancastrian Prince (5) (4,960/1960) at anchor in the Thames (top). She was the last of 11 ships built for the company at Burntisland, and arguably the final recognisably traditional ship built for Prince Line. She could be distinguished by a tall radar mast on the bridge and an absence of topmasts. Sale after just 11 years of service in 1971 saw her become *Tamara*, a name which in 1982 was shortened to *Amar*, probably for her last voyage to breakers in India. *[Furness Withy/Author's collection]*

Malvern Prince (1,459/1970) moored stern on at Malta (right) and off Newport, South Wales in April 1981 after the addition of PRINCE LINE to her hull (bottom). Sold to Vietnam in 1981 she became *Victory 1* and then *Thang Loi 1.* 'Lloyd's Register' continued to list her in July 2008. *[G.E.P. Brownell/World Ship Society Ltd.; J. and M. Clarkson collection]*

Also at Malta is *Chiltern Prince* (1,459/1970) (top). Like her sister, in 1981 she was sold to Vietnam and under various ownerships, which were probably controlled by the government, was named *Friendship* and later *Thang Loi 2.* She too was still reported to still be in existence in July 2008. *[Tom Rayner/Roy Fenton collection]*

Mendip Prince (1,459/1970) outward bound in the Channel during 1971 with a deck cargo of tractors on number 2 hatch (above). In 1974 she was renamed *Cheviot Prince* (right). Like others of the class, for a period she carried the words PRINCE LINE on her hull. Following her sale in 1979 she went to the Middle East, and has since carried the names *Rashidah, Karim, Victory 1, Manara, Nader 3, United* and *Boss.* Three of this class of four 1970-built ships appear to have survived until 2008. *[Fotoflite incorporating Skyfotos/Author's collection; J.K. Byass/Roy Fenton collection]*

Cotswold Prince (1,459/1970) also carried the line's title on her hull. Following her sale in 1979, this ship went out to the Pacific, subsequent names being Fijian and Onehunga, before reverting to Cotswold Prince at the behest of new owners in 1990. She was broken up at Mumbai in 2004. [Fotoflite incorporating Skyfotos 328159]

A brief reversion to a traditional name came with the fourth Saxon Prince (1,581/1971), although such time-honoured names were also given to the numerous ships Prince Line chartered about this time, including three Dutch-built sisters of Saxon Prince. This ship was launched for Cairn Line as Cairntrader, and reverted to this name between 1975 and 1976. Later in 1976 she was sold, and was subsequently named Adara, Andara, Parana Star, Pamela, Arana, and Karim 1. She sank at Constanta, Romania on 23rd May 2006 following a collision with the Turkish chemical tanker Zoppun (3,541/1980). [Fotoflite incorporating Skyfotos 71-5849]

The 16-knot 126-TEU container ship *Pennine Prince* (1,599/1971) leaves the builders' yard in Rotterdam for trials in 1971 (right). Ownership was formally with Pacific Maritime Services Ltd. She was renamed *Sailor Prince* in 1972 and employed on a joint service for Prince, Zim and Ellerman Lines (middle). The UK terminal was Victoria Deep Water Terminal at Greenwich, and on the outward voyages calls were made at Malta, Piraeus, Limassol, Ashdod and Haifa. Return voyages were usually direct from Israel to London, with occasional calls at Leixoes.

In 1978 she was transferred to a service involving Arab ports, and a change of name to *Soldier Prince* was thought prudent. She still ran from Victoria Deep Water Terminal, but her initial voyage took her to Esbjerg, Rotterdam, Cartagena, Valletta, Piraeus,

Limassol, Iskenderun in Turkey, Tartous in Syria, Tripoli and Beirut. She returned via Piraeus, Koper in Yugoslavia and Salerno. The photograph at the bottom taken in August 1977 suggests she also called at Gibraltar on occasions.

Sold out of the fleet in 1979, her further career was relatively short. Renamed first *Alfa*, then *Phaedra* and finally *Transporter,* she was damaged by fire at Piraeus in September 1987 and sent from there to breakers at Aliaga, Turkey. She was yet another former Prince Line ship to have her career prematurely terminated by a fire.

[Fotobureau C. Kramer/Author's collection; Fotoflite incorporating Skyfotos 340535; J. and M. Clarkson collection]

Appropriately, the last vessels built for Prince Line were completed in Newcastle-on-Tyne, from whence came its founder, James Knott. They were again gearless cellular container ships with a capacity of a modest 288 TEU, with unmanned engine rooms and bow thrusters. Alas, they were not to remain with Prince for long, and after just four years *Crown Prince* (3) (1,599/1979) moved to Manchester Liners as *Manchester Crown*. In 1985, she moved on again, and subsequently carried the names *Thai Amber*, *OOCL Advance*, *HMM Advance* and *Jin Fa*. She was demolished at Mumbai in November 1999. *[Fotoflite incorporating Skyfotos 11409]*

Royal Prince (5) (1,599/1979) was used on a Mediterranean service run jointly with Manchester Liners from terminals at Ellesmere Port and Hull and in this photograph at Malta she has mainly Manchester Liners' containers on deck. Ellerman Lines also became involved, and for a period in 1984 and 1985 *Royal Prince* ran under Ellerman colours as *City of Oporto*. Sold in 1985, subsequent names have been *Thai Jade*, *OOCL Ambition*, *Host Country*, *Jin Zhan*, *Onto Star*, *Le Yu Quan* and *Quan*, thus equalling the record set by *Mendip Prince* for the number of different names carried by a Prince Line ship. *Quan* was broken up at Chittagong in March 2007. *[Ships in Focus collection]*

Kelburne aground at Bangor. *[Author's collection]*

Kelburne in Preston Dock, probably during her ownership in the port between 1919 and 1924. The photograph was probably taken by the father of Douglas Cochrane, whose collection was left to the World Ship Society. *[World Ship Society Ltd.]*

IRON IN HER SOUL

Ian Wilson

The striking photo of a stranded steamer (opposite page, top) is taken from a glass lantern slide. Until the advent of scanning it was difficult to obtain a positive print from such a slide, which is itself a positive. When the slide was printed, I was delighted to see the name *Kelburne*. The location is recognisable as Bangor, County Down, and not just from the faint lettering 'ashore at Pickie' (a rocky section of Bangor Bay and later the site of a large outdoor bathing pool). In the background is the New or North Pier, completed in 1894 or 1895. This helps to date the incident, almost certainly to between 1894 and 1899, when the *Kelburne* left Whitehaven ownership for the north east of England and presumably no longer traded in the Irish Sea. Given her ownership in Whitehaven, it is likely she was in the coal trade to Ireland at the time of the incident, about which nothing else is known.

The *Kelburne* of 1891 was undoubtedly one of the last steam coasters to be built of iron. A quick and statistically unsound survey of around 80 steam coasters from this era showed that almost all those built of iron dated from before 1890, and only one was built after *Kelburne*, Robertson's *Zircon* of 1895. *Kelburne*'s tough construction obviously aided her return to service after an earlier stranding in March 1893 when she went ashore on the east side of the Old Head of Kinsale whilst on a short passage round the coast from Cork to Schull.

Her resilience was also called upon in the Bangor incident, after which her career continued for at least a quarter of a century until her final, fateful stranding at Port St. Mary in the Isle of Man. But no doubt there were other scrapes along the way!

Editor's note: coasters continued to be built with iron framing and steel plating during the 1890s by at least one British yard, R. Williamson and Son of Workington, who continued using the combination until the *Queens Channel* of 1894. Steel was stronger, pound for pound, than iron which meant scantlings could be reduced in thickness and therefore cost whilst maintaining strength. However, steel gave more problems with corrosion, and hulls of iron have tended to survive longer than those built with steel.

KELBURNE 1891-1924
O.N. 98655 200g 87n
114.0 x 19.6 x 8.8 feet
C. 2-cyl. by Bow, McLachlan and Co., Paisley; 35 NHP, 170 IHP.
7.1891: Completed by J. McArthur and Co., Paisley (Yard No. 67).
17.7.1891: Registered in the ownership of Peter D. Hendry, Glasgow as KELBURNE.
26.3.1893: Stranded near the Old Head of Kinsale whilst on a voyage from Cork to Schull with general cargo.
19.6.1893: Register closed.
19.1.1894: Following salvage, re-registered in the ownership of John S. Mackenzie and Co., Dublin.
15.2.1894: Sold to Robert Simpson, Whitehaven.
22.6.1899: Sold to John W. Watson, Stockton-on-Tees.
1910: Owners became Mrs. E. Watson and later A.J. Watson.
2.3.1910: Sold to James Tupman, trading as Ward and Tupman, Leith.
21.9.1911: Owners became the Steamship Kelburne Co. Ltd. (James Tupman, trading as Ward and Tupman, managers), Leith.
7.2.1917: Sold to Donald McLeod and Co., London.
19.7.1917: Sold to Steam Traders Ltd. (Vernon S. Lovell, manager), London.
31.5.1919: Sold to Joseph Gale and James Foster, Preston.
28.11.1924: Stranded alongside promenade at Chapel Bay, Port St. Mary, Isle of Man after leaving that port in heavy weather and became a constructive total loss.
4.2.1925: Register closed.

Kelburne stranded at Chapel Bay, Port St. Mary in November 1924. Although she still looks intact, her 33 years were against her, and she was declared a constructive total loss, and presumably taken away for scrap. *[Roy Fenton collection]*

Roselyne (1), the former *Poldhu*, was one of Lindsay's most successful ships. The vertically offset derricks indicate that, like many Dutch coasters, her mast was designed to hinge. *[Fotoflite incorporating Skyfotos/Douglas J. Lindsay collection]*

Rosemarkie approaching Whitby, almost certainly to load lime, an important trade for Lindsays in the 1950s and 1960s. *[Doran Brothers/Douglas J. Lindsay collection]*

W.N. LINDSAY LTD. OF LEITH
Part 2
Graeme Somner and Douglas J. Lindsay

Modernising the fleet

Up to the mid 1950s all the ships of W.N. Lindsay Ltd. were coal-burning steamers but the economics of these were becoming less and less attractive, and the last of these old style colliers, *John Evelyn*, was sold in 1957 to Channel Island interests. In 1955 the modern world caught up with the company when the first motor ship was bought. This was the *Roselyne* (1), ex-*Poldhu*, built in Holland in 1939. She was a typical small Dutchman of her time and for the company a radical departure in every way – in design, in construction (a welded hull with light scantlings) and in her propulsion. The *Roselyne* gave her new owners and crew not a few headaches before they could get to grips with this leap into the modern world, but in the end the *Roselyne* was probably the most successful ship the firm ever owned.

With the departure of the firm's steamers more ships were needed and the *Karri* was bought from Joseph Fisher and Sons Ltd. of Newry in August 1957. Although a motor ship the *Karri* was a throw-back, with the design and layout of the old steam colliers, even having forecastle-head accommodation for the deckhands. In 1958 a further motor ship was purchased, the ex-Royal Army Service Corps supply ship *Malplaquet*. After a spell in Singapore this vessel had been employed taking dangerous ammunition loaded at Cairnryan, Dumfriesshire for dumping in the Beaufort Dyke midway between Scotland and Northern Ireland. On acquisition by W.N. Lindsay she was entered on to the merchant register and renamed *Rosemarkie* (1). She was a particularly well-built and equipped little ship but unfortunately her cubic capacity and deadweight were not good and her economics were always against her. In 1962 she ran aground at Whalsay in the Shetland Isles and was extensively damaged but was considered worth repairing so continued to serve for another six years. A project in 1964 to lengthen her by twenty feet, which would have turned her into a very useful carrier, was unfortunately never carried through and she went for scrap in 1968 despite still being in excellent condition. With the *Rosemarkie* the practice of naming the ships *Rose-* became established, being borrowed from the *Roselyne* (1) which brought the name with her when acquired by Lindsay.

These three ships saw the company into the early 1960s. In 1963 W.N. Lindsay took a step backwards with the purchase of the *Roseneath*, a coal-burning steamer. This ship was substantially larger than any other ships ever owned by W.N. Lindsay at 1,500 tons deadweight, and was not

In Leith Docks barley from Australia is loaded overside from a Silver Line ship into *Karri*, which will take it to distilleries around Burghead. This was one of the last cargoes of bagged barley imported by W.N. Lindsay Ltd. *[A.G. Ingram Ltd./Douglas J. Lindsay collection]*

At Lerwick in May 1973 *Roselyne* (2) discharges bagged cement and *Rosewell* unloads fertiliser, both cargoes for Hay and Co.
[Dennis Coutts/Douglas J. Lindsay collection]

acquired for general tramping. Lindsays had by then developed a strong working relationship with Fisons the fertiliser company and the *Roseneath* was bought to service a time charter with Fisons providing a shuttle service carrying bulk fertilisers from Immingham to Leith. She did sometimes load at other ports – Goole, Ipswich, Barking on the Thames – but mostly her trade was from Immingham (where bunker coal was still readily available) to Leith. She had been built as the *Poole Harbour,* one of a class of six small colliers built to serve the power station at Poole where ship dimensions were severely limited.

In 1964 the *Roseburn* was bought. This vessel, the ex-*Thorium* of Imperial Chemical Industries, had spent her life carrying limestone from North Wales quarries to Fleetwood. Remarkably, the

The supply vessel *Malplaquet* was built for the British Army and was bought by Lindsays for conversion to a conventional coaster. She is seen on a slipway at Singapore. *[Douglas J. Lindsay collection]*

ship is shown as still trading in Turkey in 2008, over 60 years after she was built, and is worthy of a study on her own. With her acquisition W.N. Lindsay owned five ships, the second zenith of their ship owning activities after the fleet of six ships owned in 1951- 53.

In August 1966 the *Roselyne* (1) was sold to Greek owners, and the following summer the *Karri* went the same way. In the summer of 1967 the *Roseneath's* long time charter to Fisons came to an end. W.N. Lindsay Ltd. tried tramping her on the home trade markets but this was a disastrous move, with the ship at one point in early 1968 stranded in Cork for lack of bunkers. House coal by the sackfull delivered by a domestic supplier enabled the ship to get to the Bristol Channel and obtain full bunkers, but the era of the coal burner was over and the ship went to scrap at Hendrik Ido Ambacht in Holland on 12th April 1968. The *Roseneath* was the second-to-last coal burning steamer left on the UK register when scrapped, outlived by a few months only by the Aberdeen collier *Thrift* (638/1931). The *Rosemarkie*, with her special survey due, had been laid up at Granton late in 1967 and the decision was made to scrap her a couple of months after *Roseneath*, rather than go through the expense of the rigorous 20-year survey.

To fill the gap the Bristol-built and owned *Hotwells* was purchased in June 1970. Renamed *Rosewell,* this ship traded under W.N. Lindsay until 1974 when she was transferred to the Voe Shipping Co. Ltd. This company was formed as a 50:50 joint venture by Hays and W.N. Lindsay Ltd., and the *Rosewell* was registered in Lerwick. The aim of Voe Shipping was to tap into the booming oil trade in Shetland, and in particular the construction traffic for the oil terminal at Sullom Voe. But the *Rosewell* was too small and too old to make much impression on a trade which by then was drawing in substantial shipping resources; the venture never really took off and after mostly running in the two owners' own trades the *Rosewell* was sold to Greek buyers in 1977, the company being wound up a few years later.

Reorganisation

The year 1967 also saw a corporate change: W.N. Lindsay was re-organised to become a grain trading and holding company, with increasing property interests. All the marine activities, including owning the ships, were hived off to W.N. Lindsay (Shipowners) Ltd., a wholly-owned subsidiary. At the same time the Berwick activities were put into the subsidiary, W.N. Lindsay (Stevedores) Ltd.

A contrast in size: *Roselyne* (1) alongside *Roseneath* at Leith, 17th June 1966. *[Dan McDonald/Douglas J. Lindsay collection]*

This is perhaps an appropriate point to comment on how the coasting trades were organised. There tended to be one or two coaster owners in each of the more significant ports around the UK. These firms all knew each other and - while competitors for cargoes - also provided a loose support system. Each firm gave an agency service in its home port for ships of other coaster owners calling there, and often also a brokerage service. They carefully looked after each others' interests, with a common understanding of the ships' needs and activities. This agency and brokerage could be a significant part of a firm's business and provided an important network for the country's smaller ship owners to rely on.

After 1968 W.N. Lindsay's fleet was unchanged for a few years. Then, in the summer of 1973, the *Roseburn* was sold to Greek island interests, passed through various hands including a spell as the *Salvager 1* (what was she doing then, one wonders?) before being sold to Turks for whom she was still trading in 2008. To replace her the *Roselyne* (2), ex-*Pamela C,* was bought in the spring of 1973. She was another Dutch-built coaster of the classic style, economic and efficient. The *Rosemarkie* (2) ex-*Marinex III,* was bought later the same year, after carrying stone between Berwick and Newcastle for some time on charter to the road builders Tarmac.

Again, the fleet was then settled for a few years until 1977, when the *Rosewell* was sold by Voe Shipping. At much the same time the *Rosemarkie* (2) was sold to the Ramagge family of Gibraltar. Renamed *Carlizanne* under the Panamanian flag, she was used by her new owners to run a semi-liner service from North Europe to Gibraltar.

To be continued

Rosewell in dry dock at South Shields. *[Freddie Hunter/Douglas J. Lindsay collection]*

Douglas W.N. Lindsay at work, on the *Roseburn*. Note the highly polished brasswork in the wheelhouse, a sure sign of a Buckie crew. *[Douglas J. Lindsay collection]*

Fleet list part 2

12. ROSELYNE (1) 1956-1966
O.N. 164250 422g 202n
151.9 x 26.0 x 9.0 feet
Oil engine 6-cyl. 4SCSA by
Appingedammer Brons Motorenfabriek
N.V., Appingedam, Netherlands.
2.1939: Built by N.V. Scheepswerf
'Foxhol', Foxhol, Netherlands for Polpen
Shipping Co. Ltd. (Hannan, Samuel and Co.
Ltd., managers), Fowey as POLDHU.
6.1940: Captured by German forces whilst
being salvaged after being aground at Ile de
Sein, Ushant, France. Treated as a total loss
by underwriters.
1945: Recovered and bought back by
Polpen Shipping Co. Ltd.
1.1956: Acquired by W.N. Lindsay Ltd.,
Leith. She had been re-named ROSELYNE
shortly before being acquired.
8.1966: Sold to N. Mparmpas and D.
Moschovis, Salonica, Greece and renamed
ANNA.
1972: Sold to Anna I. Kalligeraki, Panama.
1976: Sold to Marisud S.p.A., Augusta, Italy
and renamed ELEUSI.
1981: Sold to Angelo Spinelli, Brindisi,
Italy.
5.1997: Deleted from 'Lloyd's Register' as
continued existence in doubt.

13. KARRI 1957-1967
O.N. 160298 354g 179n
139.6 x 23.9 x 8.8 feet
Oil engine 8-cyl. 4SCSA by Humboldt-
Deutz Motoren A.G., Koln-Deutz; Germany.
5.1942: Oil engine 6-cyl. 2SCSA by British
Auxiliaries Ltd., Glasgow; 520 BHP.
30.6.1938: Launched by Scott and Sons,
Bowling (Yard No. 347) for Newry and
Kilkeel Steamship Co. Ltd. (Joseph Fisher
and Sons Ltd., managers), Newry as
KARRI.
9.1938: Completed.
15.1.1942: Caught fire after being damaged
by a mine (a bomb according to the legend;
her starboard side was dished in by the
blast and remained so for the rest of her
life) two miles north of the Bar Light
Vessel, River Mersey while on passage
from Garston to Dublin with a cargo of
coal.
5.1942: Refitted with a British-built engine,
no spares being available to refurbish her
German-built engine.
8.1957: Acquired by W.N. Lindsay Ltd.,
Leith.
8.1967: Sold to M. Gigilinis and D.
Kalkasinas, Thessalonica, Greece.
1967: Sold to A. Latridi Brothers,
Thessalonica and renamed ATHANASIOS I.
1976: Sold to J. Palmos, Mytilone, Greece.
1977: Sold to Intership Co. Ltd., Honduras
and renamed SYLVIA.
19.5.1977: Foundered 50 miles south of
Toulon in position 42.32 north by 06.07 east
after springing a leak when engine failed in
heavy weather.

A typical Dutch coaster, although built for British owners, *Poldhu* had an adventurous life before being acquired by Lindsay (above). For Hannan, Samuel and Co. Ltd. she had taken granite blocks out to Gibraltar, returning with locust beans from North Africa. In summer months she also carried china clay to the Baltic, returning with timber, as well as working coastwise. After running aground in 1940, she spent the war in German hands, being bought back by her owners after the war. The photograph was taken on the Ouse in 1939: note the life rafts on a temporary platform amidships. *[C.A. Hill/Douglas J. Lindsay collection]*

Roselyne, formerly *Poldhu*. Note that a light signal mast has been added ahead of her funnel. *[Ships in Focus collection]*

Karri at North Pier, Fair Isle about 1960. *[Douglas J. Lindsay collection]*

Built for the rather conservative Joseph Fisher and Sons Ltd. of Newry, *Karri* was a motor ship built to a steam coaster design (above). This photograph of her during her ten years of Lindsay ownership shows her heading up the New Waterway. *[Douglas J. Lindsay collection]*

Malplaquet at Leith (right) prior to being renamed *Rosemarkie* (1). *[Douglas J. Lindsay collection]*

Rosemarkie (1) was named after a small village just north of Inverness (below). However, there is some evidence that the name originally chosen for her was *Roseneath*. *[Graeme Somner collection]*

Colorcrete, the former *Poole Harbour,* was built to carry coal from Goole to the power station at Poole (left). Bought by Lindsay and renamed *Roseneath,* she still occasionally loaded at Goole, and is seen in the Ouse under her new name (below). *[Left: J. and M. Clarkson collection, below: C. A. Hill/ Douglas J. Lindsay collection]*

14. ROSEMARKIE (1) 1958-1968
O.N. 186664 499g 218n
153.0 x 27.3 x 12.0 feet
Oil engine 8-cyl. 4SCSA by Mirrlees, Bickerton and Day, Stockport, Lancashire.
21.4.1939: Launched by Cochrane and Sons Ltd., Selby, Yorkshire (Yard No. 1199) for the Royal Army Service Corps (Water Transport) as the supply vessel MALPLAQUET.
7.1939: Completed.
2.1.1940: Delivered.
7.1958: Acquired by W.N. Lindsay Ltd., Leith, converted to a dry cargo vessel and renamed ROSEMARKIE.
9.10.1962: Stranded off Whalsay Island, Shetland Islands, but refloated with extensive damage, and subsequently repaired.
1967: Owners title now W.N. Lindsay (Shipowners) Ltd.
12.8.1968: Arrived at Inverkeithing for breaking up by T.W. Ward Ltd.

15. ROSENEATH 1963-1968
O.N. 183005 1,366g 622n
235.1 x 36.0 x 14.3 feet
T. 3-cyl by North East Marine Engineering Co. Ltd., Sunderland; 247 NHP.
16.12.1948: Launched by J. Crown and Sons Ltd., Sunderland (Yard No. 227) for British Electricity Authority (William Cory and Sons Ltd., managers), London as POOLE HARBOUR.
4.1949: Completed.
3.1959: Sold to Associated Portland Cement Manufacturers Ltd., London and renamed COLORCRETE.
1.1963: Acquired by W.N. Lindsay Ltd., Leith and renamed ROSENEATH.
1967: Owners title now W.N. Lindsay (Shipowners) Ltd.
4.1968: Broken up in Holland.

16. ROSEBURN 1964-1973
O.N. 181077 604g 284n
197.0 x 28.5 x 10.8 feet
Oil engine 7-cyl. 2SCSA by British Polar Engines Ltd., Glasgow; 520 BHP.
26.10.1946: Launched by Burntisland Shipbuilding Co. Ltd., Burntisland (Yard No. 312) for Imperial Chemical Industries Ltd., Liverpool as THORIUM.
3.1947: Completed.
7.1964: Acquired by W.N. Lindsay Ltd., Leith and renamed ROSEBURN.
1967: Owners became W.N. Lindsay (Shipowners) Ltd.

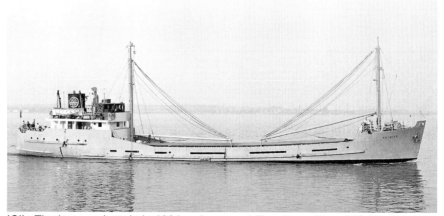

ICI's *Thorium* was bought in 1964 and renamed *Roseburn.* *[J. and M. Clarkson]*

Roseburn at Preston, her hull retaining the grey colour in which she ran for ICI as *Thorium*. *[J. and M. Clarkson]*

1.1973: Sold to Storm Compania Naviera S.A., Honduras and renamed STAVROS EMMANUEL.
1976: Renamed SALVAGER 1 and registered in Panama.
1985: Sold to Ahmet Tahsin Diker Kardesler Kollektif Sirket, Istanbul, Turkey and renamed L MEHMET DIKER.
5.1995: Sold to Ayanoglu Denizcilik ve Ticaret A.S., Istanbul and renamed DENIZ 4.
18.7.2008: Still listed by 'Lloyd's Register'.

17. ROSEWELL 1970-1977
O.N. 183679 499g 248n
163.0 x 27.1 x 11.5 feet
Oil engine 6-cyl. 4SCSA by Ruston and Hornsby Ltd., Lincoln; 540 BHP.
7.12.1949: Launched by Charles Hill and Sons Ltd., Bristol (Yard No. 358) for Osborn and Wallis Ltd., Bristol as HOTWELLS.
3.1950: Completed.
6.1970: Acquired by W.N. Lindsay (Shipowners) Ltd., Leith and renamed ROSEWELL

6.1974: Transferred to Voe Shipping Co. Ltd. (W.N. Lindsay Ltd., managers), Lerwick.
1977: Sold to Panagiotis Maidonis, Piraeus, Greece and renamed MYRSINI.
1983: Managers became Navi-Hellenic Maritime Ltd.
26.12.1996: Struck a pier at Ancona, Italy, and started to take in water. Moved to shallower water after her cargo of gypsum was discharged to allow temporary repairs to take place. No work took place and she was abandoned by her owners.

Hotwells was built for the Bristol Channel coal trade. Lindsays renamed her *Rosewell* and traded her much further afield, as the photograph of her heading for Rotterdam testifies (opposite page top). *[J. and M. Clarkson; J.K. Byass/Douglas J. Lindsay collection]*

Roselyne (2) in the New Waterway. *[Roger Sherlock]*

18. ROSELYNE (2) 1973-1979
O.N. 343114 494g 325n
189.0 x 28.2 x 11.0 feet
Oil engine 6-cyl. 4SCSA by
Appingedammer Brons, Appingedam,
Netherlands; 395 BHP.
3.9.1955: Launched by Grol's
Scheepswerven, Zuidbroek, Netherlands
(Yard No. 43) for Gebroeder de Boer,

Delfzijl, Netherlands as PLANCIUS.
11.1955: Completed.
1972: Sold to D. Cumming and Co. Ltd.,
London and renamed PAMELA C.
3.1973: Acquired by W.N. Lindsay
(Shipowners) Ltd., Leith and renamed
ROSELYNE.
6.1979: Sold to Longhaven Shipping
(Jersey) Ltd., St. Helier, Jersey.

5.1980: Transferred to Longhaven Carriers
Ltd., St. Helier.
9.1980: Sold by court order to D.J.
Lindsay Marine Ltd., Leith.
11.1980: Sold to Galaxy Shoppe
(Anguilla) Ltd., Anguilla, West Indies.
1.1982: Registered at Anguilla.
2000: Deleted from 'Lloyd's Register' as
presumed broken up.

19. ROSEMARKIE (2) 1973-1977

O.N. 339250 554g 283n
200.7 x 30.5 x 12.0 feet
Oil engine 6-cyl. 4SCSA by N.V.
Werkspoor, Amsterdam, Netherlands;
600 BHP.
6.6.1957: Launched by Scheepswerf
'Vooruitgang' van Gebroeder
Suurmeijer, Foxhol, Netherlands (Yard
No. 185).
4.9.1957: Delivered to van Nievelt
Goudriaan and Co.'s Stoomvaart
Maatschappij, Rotterdam, Netherlands
as THUBAN.
2.7.1964: Sold to I/S Lars Rej
Johansen and Knut A. Knutsen, Oslo,
Norway and renamed JOVISTA.
1966: Sold to Hakon Kragerud, Oslo
and renamed PETRO MINOR.
1968: Sold to Arensen's Rederi A/S,
Kristiansund, Norway and renamed
JOVISTA.
1970: Sold to Marine Gravel Co. Ltd.,
London and renamed MARINEX III.
10.1973: Acquired by W.N. Lindsay
(Shipowners) Ltd., Leith and renamed
ROSEMARKIE.
4.1977: Sold to Naviera Carlizanne
S.A., Panama (J.H. Ramagge,
Gibraltar, manager) and renamed
CARLIZANNE.
20.12.1985: Sailed from Gibraltar for
Puerto de Santa Maria, near Cadiz,
Spain, for breaking up.

The second *Rosemarkie* on the River Ouse (above) and at Gibraltar on 26th August 1981 (below) following her sale to local owners as *Carlizanne*. [C.A. Hill; Dave Hocquard/both Douglas J. Lindsay collection]

SOURCES AND ACKNOWLEDGEMENTS

We thank all who gave permission for their photographs to be used, and for help in finding photographs we are particularly grateful to Tony Smith, Jim McFaul and David Whiteside of the World Ship Photo Library; to Ian Farquhar, F.W. Hawks, Peter Newall, William Schell, George Scott; and to David Hodge and Bob Todd of the National Maritime Museum, and other museums and institutions listed.

Research sources have included the *Registers* of William Schell and Tony Starke, *Lloyd's Register*, *Lloyd's Confidential Index*, *Lloyd's War Losses*, *Mercantile Navy Lists*, *Marine News* and *Shipbuilding and Shipping Record*. Use of the facilities of the World Ship Society, the Guildhall Library, the National Archives and Lloyd's Register of Shipping and the help of Dr Malcolm Cooper are gratefully acknowledged. Particular thanks also to Heather Fenton for editorial and indexing work, and to Marion Clarkson for accountancy services.

Fleet in Focus: Prince Line post-war

'Fifty Years with Prince Line' by Captain R.C. Proctor (Stockwell, Ilfracombe, 1967).
'Progress of the Prince Line 1875-1949' by A.J. Henderson (Birchall, Liverpool, 1949) based on an article in 'Sea Breezes' October 1949.
'Furness Withy 1891-1991' by David Burrell (World Ship Society, Kendal, 1992)'

Sir James Knott's Confidential Instructions to Agents.
Prince Line Private Sailing Directions, 1908
'Pride of the Princes' by Norman Middlemiss (Shields Publications, Newcastle, 1988)
'Merchant Fleets: Furness Withy' by Duncan Haws (Duncan Haws, Pembroke, 2000).
Thanks also to Captain Edward Buckle, John A. Gates, E.E. Milburn, and to two photographers, the late A.J. Henderson and A.J.B. Davidson.

Shell's Former Sailing Ship Tankers

BT 110 closed registers, and Treasury file IR 82/7 at the National Archives, supplemented by 'Lloyd's Confidential Index' and published company histories. Thanks to John Naylon for supplying both the photographs of the sailing vessels and their captions

Liberty Ships on Charter to Britain

This was based on materials in the Guildhall Library, the National Archives (ADM1, 187, and 199; BT110, 381, 385, 389; and MT 40 and 59) and the Second World War 'Service Lists'. Many thanks to William Schell for help with finding the names of companies who managed the Liberties for the Ministry of War Transport.

Nigerian National Shipping Line

Thanks to John Goble for additional material.

NIGERIAN NATIONAL SHIPPING LINE LTD. Part 2
Andrew Huckett

New lines, new ships

In 1965 Nigerian National Shipping Line Ltd. (NNSL) joined with Elder Dempster and Palm Line to form the Africa Container Express Ltd. in order to introduce containerisation to the West African trade. The service used 8 x 8 x 10 feet containers made of fibreglass to help insulation.

On 1st January 1968 the conference structure was reorganised. WALCON ceased to exist and was replaced by two new conferences and NNSL became a member of both. UK and Eire services to and from West Africa became the United Kingdom-West Africa Lines Joint Service (UKWAL) whilst Continental and Scandinavian services to and from West Africa became the Continent West Africa Conference (COWAC).

In May 1968 NNSL took delivery of the first of four new ships built in Germany by Rheinstahl Nordseewerke at Emden. The *River Niger*, *River Benue*, *River Ogun* and *River Ethiope* were all named after Nigerian rivers, as were all future acquisitions. They brought the total fleet to 13 before the loss of *Oba Ovonramwen*.

The position of the fleet on 1st December 1969 was as follows:

Dan Fodio	Not known, but sailed from Sunderland on 11th December.
Oduduwa	At Rouen, having arrived from Calabar and other West African ports to Hamburg, Bremen, Rotterdam and Dunkirk and prior to sailing to Nouakchott (Mauritania), Dakar, Tema and Apapa/Lagos.
King Jaja	Probably at Port Harcourt prior to sailing for Apapa/Lagos and Calabar.
El Kanemi	At sea having called at Victoria (Cameroon), Douala and Calabar and prior to sailing to Las Palmas, Rotterdam, Amsterdam and Middlesbrough.
Oranyan	At sea having called at Warri, Sapele and Abidjan and prior to sailing to Avonmouth, Rotterdam and Tilbury.
Nnamdi Azikiwe	At sea having called at Apapa/Lagos and Takoradi and prior to sailing to Hull, Hamburg, Bremen, Rotterdam and Antwerp.
Ahmadu Bello	At sea having called at Apapa/Lagos, Takoradi and Dakar and prior to sailing to Avonmouth and Liverpool.
Herbert Macaulay	At Abidjan having called at Calabar, Apapa/Lagos and Takoradi and prior to sailing to Freetown and Dublin.

RIVER NIGER 1968-1983
Rheinstahl Nordseewerke, Emden, 1968; 7,827gt, 136.53 metres 6-cyl. 2SCSA Burmeister & Wain-type oil engine by S.A. Cockerill-Ougrée-Providence, Seraingo

The first ship built for NNSL outside the UK, *River Niger* sails from Liverpool. She was sold in 1983 to a Greek owner with an appetite for NNSL ships, S.C. Vazeos, who registered her under Ruislip Marine Co. Ltd. of Limassol and simply renamed her *River*. In the following year Vazeos moved her to Cannes Shipping Co. Ltd. Limassol of Cyprus and renamed her *Tiger*. She has since been deleted from 'Lloyd's Register' as her continued existence is in doubt. *[J. and M. Clarkson]*

RIVER BENUE 1968-1983
Rheinstahl Nordseewerke, Emden,
1968; 7,827gt, 136.53 metres
6-cyl. 2SCSA Burmeister & Wain-type
oil engine by S.A. Cockerill-Ougrée-

Providence, Seraingo
Like her sister, *River Benue* was sold in
1983 to S.C. Vazeos who renamed her
Dynasty and placed her ownership with
Dynasty Shipping Co. Ltd. of Nicosia.

She was renamed *Parrot* in 1986 just
prior to being sold to Indian breakers.
[Jean M. Otten]

River Niger	Not known but sailed Apapa/ Lagos on 21st December for Takoradi.
River Benue	At Sapele prior to sailing to Rotterdam, Hamburg and Bremen.
River Ogun	At Apapa/Lagos prior to sailing to Takoradi and Freetown.
River Ethiope	At Hamburg having called at Emden and Bremen and prior to sailing to Antwerp, Rotterdam, Rouen, Dakar, Takoradi and Las Palmas.

In 1973 the Greek *Stamatios* was purchased and renamed *Cross River*. Further acquisitions came in 1974 with the purchase of Holland America Line's *Poeldyk*, which became *River Gongola*, and the newly-built *River Hadejia* from Poland. The latter was part of an order of a class of seven for Elder Dempster and Palm Line from Polish shipbuilders. In this year NNSL also disposed of its first ship with the sale of *Dan Fodio* to Cypriot-owners. This brought the total fleet to 14 vessels, its position on 1st December 1974 being as follows:

Oduduwa	Not known.
King Jaja	At Liverpool having arrived from Dakar and Avonmouth and prior to sailing to Newport, Swansea, Dublin and Glasgow.
El Kanemi	At sea to West African ports having sailed from Liverpool and Antwerp.
Oranyan	At sea to West African ports having sailed from Tilbury, Hull, Antwerp and Amsterdam.

Nnamdi Azikiwe	Not known but arrived in Liverpool on 7th December.
Ahmadu Bello	At Bremen having arrived from Apapa/Lagos, Rotterdam and Hamburg.
Herbert Macaulay	Not known but arrived Port Harcourt on 19th December.
River Niger	In port at Calabar having arrived from Liverpool, Monrovia and Tema and prior to sailing to Tilbury.
River Benue	At Apapa/Lagos having arrived from Port Harcourt.
River Ogun	Not known but at Dawes Island (Bonny River) on 11th December.
River Ethiope	At sea having called at Port Harcourt and Tema and prior to arriving at La Palmas and the Tees.
Cross River	At sea having called at Takoradi and Las Palmas and prior to arriving at Glasgow.
River Gongola	Not known but had previously called at Freetown, Abidjan, Tema and Lome.
River Hadejia	At Apapa/Lagos having arrived from Tilbury and prior to sailing to Tilbury.

The following four years saw further reductions in the fleet with the sale for further trading of *King Jaja* and *Oduduwa* in 1975, *Oranyan* and *Herbert Macaulay* in 1976, *Cross River* in 1977 and *El Kanemi* in 1978. However, the next two years saw expansion with a total of 19 new multipurpose vessels coming from yards in South Korea and Yugoslavia. This expansion was badly timed.

By 1978 political instability, through successive military coups, and massive corruption was endemic in Nigeria.

RIVER ETHIOPE 1969-1984
Rheinstahl Nordseewerke, Emden,
1969; 7,827gt, 136.53 metres
6-cyl. 2SCSA Burmeister & Wain-type
oil engine by S.A. Cockerill-Ougrée-
Providence, Seraingo
After being laid up in Liverpool in
August 1983, *River Ethiope* was sold

the following year and renamed *Nic*
by Greenock Navigation Co. Ltd.,
Limassol (Transmed Shipping Ltd.,
Athens, managers). Renamed *Limnia*
the following year she was broken up in
Taiwan in 1986.
    The Emden-built quartet are
recalled as being fine ships but, as the

last, *River Ethiope* lacked some of the
features of her three sisters. This was
rumoured to be because the builders
were attempting to recover some of
their losses caused by picking up some
extra-contractual expenses incurred by
NNSL managers visiting Germany. *[J.*
and M. Clarkson]

As a result NNSL ended up with a fleet of vessels which it did
not need. The pattern of Nigeria's trade was changing with
imports from Asia increasing and those from the traditional
sources in the UK, USA and Europe decreasing, whilst export
cargoes were dwindling. Port congestion also played its part
thanks to the cement crisis which resulted in large surcharges
on the cost of freight (see 'Record' 38).

    There were other problems. In an article entitled
'The Nigerian Shipping Industry', the Nigerian writer Funke
Agbor commented: 'Shipping trade in Nigeria has been
dominated for the most part by foreign shipping. Statistics
show that, even during its glory days, the NNSL, together
with a few other Nigerian carriers, carried a mere eleven per
cent of the total volume of Nigerian traffic and earned less
than nine per cent of the total freight revenue between 1978
and 1980. This was in spite of Nigeria being responsible
for seventy per cent of the total trade traffic of the West and
Central sub-region.' The figures quoted did not take into
account the amount of goods carried on the ships for the
crews' own account. Electrical goods and secondhand tyres
were commonly to be found in abundance on board and
would be sold once the ships reached Nigerian ports.

    With the departure of *River Gongola* in 1979, and
taking into account all the new buildings, NNSL possessed
a total of 26 ships by the end of 1980. At the start of the
decade the NNSL fleet was more or less still maintaining
the same trade pattern of five years previous – West Africa
to UK and North West Europe with occasional calls in the
Mediterranean. However, in the first part of the 1980s this
pattern began to change with visits to ports in the Far East,
Canada, the Baltic and the USSR.

    In the last months of 1984 and early 1985 three
ships were trading to the Far East. *River Majidun* left

Apapa on 29th November and anchored in Singapore
Roads on 22nd December. Early in the New Year calls
were made at Hong Kong, Keelung, Yokohama, Kobe,
Kakogawa and Kure. *River Gurara* made calls at
Singapore, Hong Kong, Fukuyama, Kobe, Yokohama,
Busan, Inchon, Kure and Keelung, while *River Ngada*
called at Singapore, Yokohama, Hitachi, Nagoya,
Kakogawa, Kobe, Fukuyama, Busan, Keelung and Hong
Kong. On the other side of the world *River Guma* arrived
at Quebec on 18th December 1984 from Liverpool, while
River Jimine was alongside in Quebec from 13th to 28th
January the following year having arrived from Antwerp.
On 16th February *River Adada* arrived in Montreal from
Hamburg. Other ships loaded components for a Soviet-
built steel works near Warri in the ports of Murmansk,
Leningrad and Klaepida.

    However, despite this widening of trade, the
1980s saw the beginnings of a steady decline in the fleet as
older tonnage went. *Nnamdi Azikiwe* and *Ahmadu Bello*
were sold in 1981, *River Niger* and *River Benue* in 1983,
River Ogun and *River Ethiope* in 1984 and *River Hadejia*
in 1986.

Claims and arrests
The year 1986 proved a bad one for the company. In
February a Hong Kong shipping company, Afea Line Ltd.,
made a claim against NNSL for more than £7 million in
respect of demurrage arising from the charter of about 10
vessels to the company the previous year. NNSL claimed
it was only acting as agent for the transport transaction
which saw the ships carry Nigerian government cargo
on behalf of the Nigerian National Supply Company.
The claim led to the arrest of five NNSL vessels in five

RIVER GONGOLA 1974-1979
Schiffswerft August Pahl, Hamburg, 1964; 5,341gt, 125.89 metres 6-cyl. 2SCSA Burmeister & Wain-type oil engine by Fried. Krupp Maschinenfabriken GmbH, Essen Launched in August 1962 for Holland American Lijn as *Poeldyk,* she was laid up prior to being completed in October 1964. Transferred to Scheepvaart Maatschappij Trans-Oceaan B.V. in 1973 she was acquired by NNSL the following year. She is seen at Avonmouth on 17th May 1974. In 1979 she was sold to Candleford Shipping Co. Ltd., Cyprus (Denval Marine Consultants Ltd., London) and renamed *Mikelden* and in 1983 she passed to COSCO to become *Su Long.* She was renamed *Hu Gui 9* in 1991 with Haida Shipping Co. Ltd. as owners. Sold in 1997 to unspecified owners and renamed *Hua Jie* she has since been deleted from 'Lloyd's Register' as her continued existence is in doubt. *[J. and M. Clarkson collection]*

European ports – Antwerp, Rotterdam, Liverpool, Rouen and Dublin.

Later in the year *River Ogbese* was arrested in Liverpool over a claim for £148,700 from Marine Industrial Hydraulics Ltd. for repairs, while *River Maje* was detained at Felixstowe over a claim for £418,000 from the United Mersey Supply Company in respect of supplies and provisions to the company. *River Maje* was later moved to Tilbury to free the berth at Felixstowe. But once these claims had been settled *River Ogbese* was again arrested on behalf of Tyne Shiprepair Ltd. over a claim for £97,500 relating to a routine dry docking of one of the company's ships.

In August *River Rima* was arrested in Liverpool over a claim by owners of cargo on board one of the previously arrested vessels. She was further arrested pending settlement of claims for £132,000 by Plypano Ltd. relating to repairs and a damaged cargo claim by Tiphook Container Rental Co. Ltd. The hope was expressed that all amounts owing to creditors would be settled by the end of October. The financial situation of NNSL was blamed on the severe reduction in cargo movements from Europe to Nigeria which had led to a considerable drop in revenue. NNSL applied to the Nigerian government for a grant to settle all the company's debts.

By November it was reported that NNSL had suspended all calls at European ports by its vessels due to fears that they could be detained to cover unpaid bills. In fact, NNSL vessels had not been operating in the UK/West Africa Lines joint service since August when it was agreed that NNSL sailings would be covered by other members of the conference. The company's indebtedness amounted to more than $9 million which was eventually settled by the Nigerian Transport Ministry.

Of this period Funke Agbor further commented: 'Despite the boom in the 1970s and 1980s, and despite being able to point to membership of five conference lines, the government's massive investment in shipping failed dismally.' To try to arrest this, and in recognition of its failure as an import-dependent economy to take advantage of global sea trade and its failure to develop national carriers in addition to the failing NNSL, in 1987 the Nigerian government set up the National Maritime Authority to implement a national shipping policy. One of the provisions of this policy was the reservation of a minimum of 50% carriage rights in favour of Nigerian carriers. Another was the establishment of a Ship Acquisition and Building Fund to assist Nigerians in the development and expansion of a national fleet. Ultimately, the efforts of the National Maritime Authority were unsuccessful and the Ship Acquisition and Building Fund was suspended in 1996 when beneficiaries were unable to repay their loans.

On 26th February 1989 tragedy overtook the *River Gurara.* Whilst on passage from West Africa to Dublin and Liverpool she suffered an engine failure in violent storm conditions and sank off Cape Espichel, about 20 miles from Lisbon with the loss of 18 members of the crew. She was carrying a cargo of containers with cocoa and wood in bulk.

River Ogbese found herself in trouble in India where she arrived on 2nd June 1989 under charter to a Nigerian exporter. After the exporter reneged on his contract with an Indian importer the ship was arrested and was not released until September 1991. The year 1989 also saw the sale of five ships, all just ten years old, the South Korean-built *Rivers Jimini, Kerawa, Rima, Aboine* and *Guma.*

The positions of the remaining 13 ships on 1st December 1989 were:

River Adada	At Tilbury having arrived from Rotterdam and Antwerp prior to sailing to Freetown, Monrovia, Tema and Apapa/Lagos.
River Mada	At Apapa/Lagos having arrived on 5th October.
River Oli	At sea having sailed from Apapa/Lagos, Tema, Freetown and Banjul and prior to arriving at Tilbury on 5th December.
River Asab	At Antwerp having arrived on 13th October from Apapa/Lagos, Takoradi, Abidjan, Dublin and Avonmouth.
River Oji	At Dublin having arrived from Tema, Takoradi, Abidjan and prior to sailing to Antwerp, Hamburg and Rotterdam.
River Andoni	At Rotterdam having arrived from Apapa/Lagos and Port Harcourt and prior to sailing to Le Havre, Hamburg and Antwerp.
River Majidun	At Port Harcourt having arrived from Tilbury, Freetown, Monrovia, Tema and Apapa/Lagos prior to returning to Apapa/Lagos and Tema.
River Osse	At Apapa/Lagos having arrived on 12th October from Singapore and Lome.
River Oshun	At Takoradi having sailed from Apapa/Lagos and Port Harcourt prior to sailing for Tilbury, Hamburg and Antwerp.
River Ogbese	At Bombay having arrived 8th November from Magdalla on the river Tapti (India) having previously been in port in Bombay between 2nd June and 19th September.
River Maje	At sea having sailed from Hamburg, Antwerp, Tilbury and Banjul and prior to arriving at Takoradi, Tema, Apapa/Lagos and Port Harcourt.
River Ngada	At sea having sailed from Apapa/Lagos, Abidjan, Monrovia and Las Palmas.
River Ikpan	At Tilbury having arrived from Takoradi and Freetown and prior to sailing to Hamburg and Antwerp before returning to Tilbury.

As the 1990s progressed the NNSL fleet was beset by mechanical failures, class disputes and seized and arrested ships. In 1991 *River Oshun* was laid up. In 1993 *River Oji* was detained in Antwerp while *River Asab* was arrested in Dunkirk. *River Ngada* suffered a fire in her accommodation while at anchor awaiting cargo in Singapore and was subsequently arrested pending payment of the salvage bill. She remained at the anchorage until August 1994 when she was sold, repaired at the Keppel Shipyard and finally sailed from Singapore for her new owners on 6th December.

In Hong Kong *River Majidun* was arrested following alleged non-payment of bills to a German ship repair company. On being released from arrest on settlement of the US$300,000 she was further detained over a claim regarding damaged cargo. 'Lloyd's Weekly Casualty Reports' noted: 'The problems for NNSL seem to be escalating as the vessel has not received any food stores since the last week of May. Ratings have confirmed they have not been paid since April and there is little or no food or money on board.'

RIVER JIMINI 1979-1989

Hyundai Heavy Industries Co. Ltd., Ulsan, 1979; 10,985gt, 147.28 metres 6-cyl. 2SCSA Burmeister & Wain-type oil engine by Mitsui Engineering and Shipbuilding Co. Ltd., Tamano
Photographed on the Tees on 2nd July 1981, *River Jimini* was the first of 11 new buildings from the Hyundai yard at Ulsan. On 28th February 1986, while manoeuvring before berthing at Owendo, Gabon, she came into contact with the French bulk carrier *Andre Delmas* (14,555/1976), which was moored loading floating logs, and took on a list to starboard. After berthing the list increased to 30 degrees. She was eventually pumped out and a cement box fitted over the damaged area. She stayed in the fleet for just 10 years before being sold in 1989 to Annico Maritime Inc. S.A., Monrovia but under the Greek flag, with N. and E. Leondaras of Piraeus as managers, and renamed *Enarxis*. Sold a number of times she

was renamed *Venezia* in 1998, *Elena X* in 2000, and *Serena I*, *Essco Ploes*, *Serena I* and *Igen Erena* all in 2001. She was broken up the same year by Indian breakers at Alang. [Author]

1994 was another bad year for the company. *River Andoni* was detained at Ellesmere Port, *River Adade* in Hamburg and both *River Mada* and *River Ikpan* at Tilbury. The *Rivers Osse*, *Oshun* and *Ngada* were all sold and *River Oli* was laid up in the Bonny River.

On 3rd April while at anchor in Las Palmas Roads *River Majidun*, having been released from detention in Hong Kong, went aground. After her cargo of empty containers had been discharged she was towed out to sea and sunk on 30th May. To provide accommodation for the crew and act as provision vessel for *River Majidun*, NNSL sent *River Ogbese* to Las Palmas where she was arrested by the port authority as collateral for services rendered to *River Majidun* and whose maintenance cost had not been settled by NNSL. *River Ogbese* was eventually released and sailed from Las Palmas on 2nd April 1995.

Due to its crippling debts the Nigerian National Shipping Line Ltd. went into liquidation in August 1995 with its remaining ships going into lay up at the inland port of Sapele, all unseaworthy due to lack of maintenance. In

1996 the *Rivers Adada*, *Mada*, *Oji* and *Asab* were sold, while the remaining four ships, *Rivers Oli*, *Ogbese*, *Maje* and *Ikpan* went in 2001.

Despite the failure of the NNSL, the Nigerian government announced the formation of a new national shipping company, Nigerian Unity Line, floated by the National Maritime Authority. It was set up to undertake deep-sea transportation of wet cargo, ocean transportation of bulk cargo, coastal tanker services, storage and warehousing, complete agency services, freight forwarding and customs clearance. In the event the new company only acquired one ship, the container ship *Resilient* from a shipyard in Poland, which it renamed *Abuja* on its completion in October 1995. By 2002 *Abuja* was detained in Sri Lanka for the settlement of salaries, allowances and other logistics needed for the vessel's maintenance. The vessel was released on 14th February 2003 on payment into court of a guarantee of US$500,000 and later that year was sold.

In August 2005 the Nigerian government announced that it intended to sell Nigerian Unity Line, a company with a shipping licence but no vessel.

RIVER MAJE 1980-2001
Brodogradiliste i Tvornica Dizel Motora 'Split', Split, 1980; 13,167gt, 174.96 metres
6-cyl. 2SCSA Sulzer-type oil engine by R.O. Tvornica Dizel Motora '3 Maj', Rijeka
In December 1984, while in Flushing Roads awaiting permission to proceed to Antwerp from Hamburg, she fouled

a mooring buoy with her propeller and while swinging around on the ebb tide dragged her anchor with her engine refusing to go astern. She was taken in tow to the Sloehaven where the fouled buoy was removed from her propeller and she was able to proceed to Antwerp. In July 1986 she was arrested at Felixstowe in respect of a claim by United Mersey Supply Company

for supplies and provisions. On 20th February 1990, when arriving at Tilbury and swinging with tug assistance in Northfleet Hope, she had engine failure and collided with the container ship *Australian Venture* (43,878/1977) lying alongside Northfleet Hope Container Terminal. Laid up at Sapele in 1995, she was sold to Indian breakers in 2001 and broken up at Alang. *[Author's collection]*

RIVER OGUN 1968-1984

Rheinstahl Nordseewerke, Emden, 1968; 7,827gt, 136.53 metres
6-cyl. 2SCSA Burmeister & Wain-type oil engine by S.A. Cockerill-Ougrée-Providence, Seraingo

The third of the German-built quartet, *River Ogun* was photographed at Liverpool on 8th April 1973 with Lever Brothers' barges alongside, loading vegetable oil for Bromborough (top). *River Ogun* was sold in 1984 as *Shogun* to Epping Marine Co. Ltd. of Nicosia. Sold again the same year to Fairview Navigation Co. Ltd., also of Cyprus, and renamed *Fairview*, she was further renamed *Fame* the following year prior to being demolished by Pakistani breakers. In the middle photograph her name has been abbreviated to *Ogun*. *[Roy Fenton; Louis Bosschart]*

CROSS RIVER 1973-1977

Astilleros de Cadiz, Cadiz, 1964; 6,044gt, 127.67 metres
5-cyl. 2SCSA Sulzer-type oil engine by Empresa Nacional 'Elcano', Valencia

Completed for Norwegian owners A/S I.M.A. (Karl J.B. Staubo, Oslo, managers) as *Ima Sam* she was renamed *Sundale* the following year for a Saguenay charter. Sold in 1970 to Faircape Steamship Corporation of Piraeus and renamed *Stamatios*, she became *Iran Sepah* in 1972 and *Stamatios* in 1973. Bought in 1973, *Cross River* was quite unsuited to NNSL trades, and as the ultimate irony could not even load at Calabar, the port on the river after which she was named. She was only acquired as a result of some lavish hospitality by her former owners.

Always unpopular with both seagoing and shore staff, she lasted with NNSL for just four years before she was sold to Greek owners Smirna Shipping Co. S.A., Panama (Deepdene Maritime Co. S.A. (Christos Papahadjopoulos), Athens, managers) and was renamed *Azalea*. Sold in 1981 and renamed *Aikaterini* she went to Turkish breakers in 1989 to be demolished at Aliaga. *[FotoFlite 280537]*

RIVER HADEJIA 1974-1986

*Stocznia Szczecinska, Szczecin, 1974;
9,389gt, 145.88 metres*
*6-cyl. 2SCSA Sulzer-type oil engine by
H. Cegielski, Poznan*
Originally ordered by Elder Dempster
Lines *River Hadejia* was sold to NNSL
while building. *River Hadejia* had more
than her share of accidents. On 12th
December 1983 while manoeuvring
she was in collision at Apapa with the
East German *Arendsee* (5,650/1978)
which was secured alongside. On 31st
December 1984 she grounded in the
River Seine at the end of a voyage from

Apapa/Lagos to Rouen, being refloated
the following day. Five weeks later,
on 9th February, she sustained slight
damage in a collision with the Greek
Sea Tide (9,810/1971) at Lagos. On
20th January 1986 a fire broke out
in the accommodation while lying at
Hamburg which destroyed two cabins
and led to nine of the crew being
hospitalised with smoke poisoning.
Later in the year she was sold to North
Star Maritime Ltd. of Bahamas (V.
Ships, Monte Carlo, managers) and
renamed *Green Lagoon*. The following
year she was sold to Cosmic Shipping

and Trading Corporation of Bahamas,
under the management of Norse
Management (UK) Ltd. of Colchester,
and renamed *Gulf Liberty*. In 1988 she
passed into the ownership of L. and M.
Shipping Pte. Ltd. of Singapore and was
renamed *LM Noble Lady*. Changing
hands again in 1990 to owners
associated with Orient Express Lines
Inc. of Dubai she was renamed *Ganges*
and *Orient Ganges* in 1991. She went
to Indian breakers at Alang in 1999.
[FotoFlite 266740]

RIVER ADADA 1979-1996

*Brodogradiliste i Tvornica Dizel Motora
'Split', Split, 1979; 13,165gt, 174.96
metres*
*6-cyl. 2SCSA Sulzer-type oil engine
by R.O. Tvornica Dizel Motora '3 Maj',
Rijeka*
River Adada was the first of the
Yugoslavian new buildings. On 17th
March 1984 she hit rocky ground during
a passage from Klaipeda to Warri via
Kiel causing some hull damage. In
October 1987 she was arrested at
Tilbury in respect of a claim by Tyne
Shiprepair Ltd. relating to general
repairs to *River Jimini*. In March
1994 she was detained in Hamburg
and eventually sold in 1996 to Power
Shipping S.A., St. Vincent and the
Grenadines and became the second
former NNSL ship to be renamed *River*.
Quickly passing into the ownership
of Mediterranean Victory Marine
Ltd. of Limassol (Jay Management

Corporation, Piraeus, managers)
she was renamed *Axion I*. In 2004
she was sold to owners associated
with Prominent Shipping Services of
Chittagong and renamed *Leonis*. In
2007 she was sold again but without

change of name to a British Virgin
Islands-based company with Austin
Navigation Singapore Pte. Ltd. as
managers. The photograph was taken
on the Thames in June 1990.
[C.L. Reynolds]

RIVER OJI 1979-1996

Brodogradiliste i Tvornica Dizel Motora 'Split', Split, 1979; 13,165gt, 174.96 metres
6-cyl. 2SCSA Sulzer-type oil engine by R.O. Tvornica Dizel Motora '3 Maj', Rijeka

While anchored off Yokohama on 12th February 1987 *River Oji's* anchor dragged in strong winds causing her to collide with two Japanese coasters, *Yasaka* (495/1977) and *Fukuyoshi Maru* (198/1977). On 12th July 1990 she sustained hull damage while lying alongside a berth at Malta Drydocks when hit by the Greek tanker *Nicholas* (56,988/1974) which was undocking. Arrested in January 1993 in Antwerp as a result of non-payment of outstanding debts by NNSL, she was not released until July 1996. She was described as being 'in such poor condition that she is a danger to navigation', but still found a buyer in the shape of Falcon Marine Corporation (Evermarine Private Ltd., Karachi, managers) who renamed her *Falconzord* under the St. Vincent flag. She went to Chinese breakers in 1999. *[Jean M. Otten]*

RIVER MAJIDUN 1979-1994

Brodogradiliste i Tvornica Dizel Motora 'Split', Split, 1979; 13,161gt, 174.96 metres
6-cyl. 2SCSA Sulzer-type oil engine by R.O. Tvornica Dizel Motora '3 Maj', Rijeka

On 6th March 1984, when berthing at Port Harcourt after arriving from Douala, *River Majidun* was in collision with the German container ship *Usaramo* (20,360/1982). In February 1986 while at Liverpool she was one of five NNSL vessels arrested in various ports in respect of a claim by Afea Line Ltd. of Hong Kong, relating to demurrage arising from the charter of vessels to the line. On 23rd April 1986 she sustained light damage when in collision with the French oil/lpg tanker *Petro Soulac* (5,841/1963) while manoeuvering at Douala. The following month she sustained minor damage whilst on a ballast passage from Singapore to Japan when in collision with the trawler *Tung Ying No. 11*. In April 1989 whilst on passage from the Ivory Coast to Dublin she lost her steering gear in heavy weather in the Bay of Biscay and was taken into Santander for repairs. In 1993 she was detained in Hong Kong on behalf of a German ship repair company but subsequently released. Her end came on 30th May 1994 when she was scuttled at sea off Las Palmas following grounding the previous month. She is shown in Liverpool in January 1989. *[Ambuscade Marine Photography 89/5/8]*

RIVER ABOINE 1979-1989

Hyundai Heavy Industries Co. Ltd., Ulsan, 1979; 10,985gt, 147.52 metres
6-cyl. 2SCSA Burmeister & Wain-type oil engine by Mitsui Engineering and Shipbuilding Co. Ltd., Tamano

After ten years in the NNSL fleet *River Aboine* was sold to Aerobell (Nigeria) Ltd. with Brawal Shipping Line of Apapa as managers and renamed *Ndoni River*, as photographed in the North Sea in 1996. Sold in 1999 to Ballito Bay Ltd. of Malta (Team Fuel Corporation, Piraeus, managers) she was renamed *Megaluck*. Sold in 2003, she was broken up at Alang by Bharat Shipbreakers Corporation. *[C.L. Reynolds]*

RIVER GURARA 1980-1989

Brodogradiliste i Tvornica Dizel Motora 'Split', Split, 1980; 13,194gt, 174.96 metres 6-cyl. 2SCSA Sulzer-type oil engine by R.O. Tvornica Dizel Motora '3 Maj', Rijeka

On 5th March 1984 *River Gurara* ran aground in the River Seine while on passage from Apapa/Lagos to Rouen but refloated under her own power. Just over a year later, on 18th March 1985, she was in collision with the French container ship *Therese Delmas* (30,750/1983) at Lagos. It was third time unlucky, as on 26th February 1989 she was overwhelmed in stormy weather following engine failure off the coast of Portugal with the loss of 18 of her passengers and crew. *[Author]*

RIVER IKPAN 1980-2001

Hyundai Heavy Industries Co. Ltd., Ulsan, 1980; 13,363gt, 167.32 metres 6-cyl. 2SCSA Burmeister & Wain-type oil engine by Mitsui Engineering and Shipbuilding Co. Ltd., Tamano

The last ship built for NNSL, *River Ikpan* was arrested at Liverpool in July 1984 in respect of a claim for £51,000 from ships riggers Coubro and Scrutton Ltd. for services to the vessel. In January 1994 she was arrested at Tilbury in respect of unpaid repairs to *River Adada* but was released the following month. Laid up at Sapele in September 1995, she was sold to Indian breakers in April 2001 and demolished at Alang. *[J. and M. Clarkson collection]*

LIBERTY SHIPS ON CHARTER TO BRITAIN
Part 1: Introduction
John de S. Winser

Plans for the division of responsibilities between the USA and Britain were agreed between President Roosevelt and Prime Minister Churchill in late 1941/early 1942 and these included concentrating energies on the activities which each country was best qualified to carry out. In the realm of cargo ship construction, it was clearly illogical to move large quantities of raw materials eastwards across the Atlantic for use by the British shipbuilding industry, then to despatch the completed vessels in ballast to the United States to load their cargoes, when the resources and techniques for the construction of standard merchant ships in record time were on hand in the USA. Consequently, it was decided that the US would be the predominant merchant shipbuilding area, while Britain concentrated primarily, but certainly not exclusively, on the building of combat vessels.

As a result of war losses and despite new building, the British merchant fleet, which had totalled over 17 million gross tons in September 1939, had declined to less than 15 million by March 1943. This had created a pool of some 10,000 trained personnel who were available to man any ships constructed in American yards and the US President therefore directed his War Shipping Administration to transfer to the Red Ensign, on their completion, 200 ocean-going cargo vessels of the Liberty type for temporary wartime duty on bareboat charter. Delivery of these 7,000grt, 11-knot mass-produced ships was to be at the rate of at least 15 per month and the ships were especially needed to cover the lack of British tonnage of the right type for cargo movements to operational areas in the Indian Ocean region. The arrangement agreed was the best that the British government could reach. Although the Americans were unwilling to transfer the ships permanently at that time, the British hoped that they might do so at the end of the war but this was never publicly stated. However, in August 1943, the possibility of this greatly exercised US newspaper editors, who queried the right of the President to give away millions of tons of shipping which 'our British friends' would then use in competition with the US merchant marine.

The agreement between the US and British governments was that the vessels would remain under the British flag until no later than six months after the termination of the war; that they would be manned, victualled, navigated, operated and maintained in a thoroughly efficient state and that they would be redelivered on the termination of service, with an estimate of the cost of restoration to their original condition, fair wear and tear excepted. No ships were permitted to be regarded as constructive total losses without the consent of the USA. The US unions denounced the plan on the grounds that, as there was no shortage of American seamen, there was no reason for the vessels not to sail under the US flag. For this reason, the US Administration went out of its way to stress to the American public that the ships remained US property

and, to diffuse union tension, Britain agreed that, for their first outward voyages from the USA, the ships would be operated by American lines.

British crews sent out to man the vessels were largely under the impression that they were to bring the ships back to the UK, whereas in reality most were loading in the USA for ports in the Mediterranean, Persian Gulf and Indian Ocean. The crew for *Samdak*, for example, signed on in Liverpool in September 1943, joined their ship at Baltimore and many of the men did not set foot in Britain until the vessel reached Avonmouth in April 1945. During this time, *Samdak* made three eastbound and two westbound crossings between North America and the central and eastern Mediterranean; sailed on two operational assignments from Naples in support of the Allied landings in the south of France and spent six months moving military cargo between ports in Egypt, Italy and Greece. When the British National Union of Seamen became aware of these extended voyages, it lost little time in claiming that, as the ships were American and being employed to a large extent between North America and other areas in the world, their crews were entitled to the higher American scales of pay. Dissatisfaction amongst the seamen was evident from the large number of last-minute desertions amongst those sent to the USA. The crew for *Samuta* signed on in London on 16th September 1943; their ship was delivered at Baltimore on 12th November and the crew boarded four days later. Fully loaded, the vessel was ready to sail for Egypt on 21st November but, by this time, two engine room greasers were absent and only one replacement could be found. Consequently, *Samuta* missed her convoy and it was not until 2nd December that she was fully manned and ready to join a transAtlantic convoy. Deserters were quite prepared to accept punishment rather than to undertake protracted voyages resulting in long absences from home. As a result, great efforts were made to route ships to the UK at the earliest opportunity to dispel the idea that they were based in the USA and, from February 1944, a number were directed to British ports on their maiden voyages.

The ships were constructed at eight US yards, with the total from each being indicated below. On the east coast these yards were: Bethlehem Fairfield at Baltimore, Maryland, 104; New England Shipbuilding at Portland, Maine, 29; J.A. Jones Construction at Brunswick, Georgia, 12; Southeastern Shipbuilding at Savannah, Georgia, 4; North Carolina Shipbuilding at Wilmington, 2 (total 151). On the west coast the yards were: California Shipbuilding at Los Angeles, 17; Permanente Metal at Richmond, San Francisco, 8 and Oregon Ship Building at Portland, 6 (total 31). Crews for the first 20 ships reached the USA in July 1943 and the first vessel to be handed over, on 17th July, was *Samholt*, followed by *Sambridge*, *Sampler* and *Samson* on the 21st, *Samaritan* two days later and *Samovar* on the 30th. All six were products of the west coast yards, where,

The newly-built *Samuta* experienced a number of desertions amongst her seamen when they discovered she was not, as they expected, due to be delivered directly to a British port but was bound for Egypt.

There were several themes to the second element of the names of the 'Sams', the one used here being an abbreviation of the name of an American state.

In 1947 *Samuta* was acquired by her managers, Andrew Weir and Co., and renamed *Kelvinbank* in the ownership of

Bank Line Ltd. Her career was short: she was wrecked on Ocean Island in the Pacific during January 1953. *[John McRoberts/J. and M. Clarkson]*

because their main defensive armament consisted only of one 4-inch, one 12-pounder and six Oerlikons, the ships could present on the loading berth only a couple of days after delivery. Those with cargo from North America to India sailed independently across the Pacific, usually calling only at Hobart in Tasmania. *Samaritan* was the first of four ships directed to Chilean ports to load nitrate for Egypt: three then made Wellington their first port of call and all four put into Fremantle and Aden. The ships built on the east coast joined convoys to combat zones and any extra defensive armament resulted in delays between delivery and readiness to load cargo.

Naming

The initial ships were launched bearing names selected by the Americans but a British decision that it would be advantageous to preserve the identity of the vessels as a group resulted in the allocation of names with a 'Sam' prefix and the first 95 had their American names changed when handed over. This arrangement did not meet with the approval of all those associated with the original name and, in seven instances, it became necessary to reverse this naming process. For instance, *Samwyo* was christened *Adolph S. Ochs*, in honour of the founder of the New York Times newspaper, at a ceremony performed by his daughter, Mrs Sulzberger Ochs, who was also the wife of the current publisher. Although this lady was quite content for the ship to operate under the Red Ensign, she was concerned about the name change and requested that the original be restored. This was agreed and, having sailed from Baltimore as *Samwyo*, the ship then reverted to her original name of *Adolph S. Ochs*. The other six vessels which did likewise were *Sambuff* to *Frank A. Vanderlip*, after arriving at Suez in January 1944; *Samariz* to *John J. McGraw* after nine months' service; *Samoine* to *Edward Bruce* and *Samvard* to *Ammla*, on completion of their outward maiden voyages to

Egypt. *Ben H. Miller*'s logbook was prepared in the name *Samroan* but changed just before departure, with the result that neither she nor *Frederick Banting*, allocated the name *Samspey*, saw service under their 'Sam' names. A decision was made not to reallocate the names *Samroan* and *Samspey* to future vessels and that the proposed *Samsula* would be dropped to avoid any confusion with the nearly similar *Samsuva*. During their voyages from Baltimore to Port Said, *Samara* was renamed *Samshire* and *Samora* became *Sampenn*. Prior to the start of her maiden voyage, *Samore*'s name was switched to *Samdel* and, after 11 months' service, *Samwharfe* was selected as replacement for *Sambur*, a name already held by a Great Western Railway cargo ship. One of the ships named by the Americans was *Louis C. Tiffany*: she was due to become *Samjack* but, before delivery, caught fire and in consequence was scrapped. Another vessel, given the name *Samdaring*, was allocated as a replacement and the name *Samjack* was utilised later. To avoid the need for future name changes, from December 1943 the War Shipping Administration agreed that the vessels for Britain would be assigned their 'Sam' names from the start and lists of British names were therefore submitted for the remainder of the fleet.

When *Samlamu* left Baltimore for Karachi on 12th July 1944, she was the 182nd and last Liberty ship to enter Red Ensign service. The total had been reduced to 182 to compensate for the allocation of 13 vessels to serve as Landing Ships Infantry (Large) for the Normandy landings, sailing under the Red Ensign with the 'Weapon' names *Anvil, Arquebus, Battleaxe, Broadsword, Crossbow, Cutlass, Gauntlet, Halberd, Javelin, Lance, Mace, Rapier* and *Spearhead*, prefixed by *Empire*. The remaining five places were Liberty ships adapted for heavy repair duty and intended to serve as HM Auxiliary Repair Ships *Assistance, Diligence, Dutiful, Faithful* and *Hecla*. Only the first two were actually transferred to the Royal Navy

Sambuff was one of seven British-allocated Liberties which reverted to her originally allocated name when the sponsors objected to the change, after one voyage becoming *Frank A. Vanderlip* as seen here. The gentleman concerned had been a journalist, a banker and one time Assistant Secretary to the US Treasury, and his widow requested that the ship revert to his name.

In April 1948 she returned to US ownership and spent almost 20 years in the Wilmington Reserve Fleet before being towed away to be broken up at Kearny, New Jersey in May 1967. *[Ships in Focus collection]*

and they were allocated to the British Pacific Fleet in 1945, the first reaching Sydney that August, before later moving to Singapore, with *Diligence* following shortly afterwards and being based at Hong Kong. The British hoped that these 18 vessels would be extra to the 200 vessels originally proposed but, when this proved not to be the US intention, gratitude for the 182 overcame any inclination to query the total with the Americans.

Management

The ships were allotted by the British Ministry of War Transport for management by companies best able to provide crews. The first 100 went to liner companies and the remainder were divided equally between tramp and liner companies, the resulting totals being as follows: Alfred Holt 13; Cayzer, Irvine 12; Andrew Weir 9; Cunard White Star 8; Royal Mail 7; Ellerman's Wilson 5; Prince Line 5; Wm. Thomson 5; Union-Castle 5; Blue Star 4; Brocklebank 4; Ellerman and Bucknall 4; Ellerman and Papayanni 4; Hain 4; Lamport and Holt 4; Henderson 4; Houlder 4; New Zealand Shipping 4; Port Line 4; B. and S. Shipping 3; Donaldson 3; Haldin and Philipps 3; Moss Hutchison

3; P. & O. 3; Reardon Smith 3; S. and J. Thompson 3; Anchor Line 2; T. and J. Harrison 2; Mungo Campbell 2; E.R. Management 2; Elder Dempster 2; Furness, Withy 2; Glen Line 2; J. and C. Harrison 2; Headlam 2; Lyle Shipping 2; Orient Steam Navigation 2; Ropner 2; Shaw, Savill 2; Westcott and Laurance 2; and 1 each to Bolton Steam Shipping; Booth; Bowring; City Line; Common Brothers; Counties Ship Management; Dodd, Thomson; Elders and Fyffes; General Steam; Hall Line; Charles Hill and Sons; Hogarth; Kaye; McCowen and Gross; Morel; John Morrison and Son; George Nisbet; Pacific Steam; Evan Thomas Radcliffe; Joseph Robinson and Sons; Runciman; E.J. Sutton; Trinder, Anderson and Watts, Watts. As noted in the list below, from 1946 management of several vessels was re-allocated, mainly those originally with Orient and Cayzer, Irvine (the latter eventually buying two of those it had relinquished). This change added David Alexander; Chellew; Dalgleish; Dene Shipping; Dunlop; Maclay, McIntyre; Seager; Strick and Strubin to the list of managers. In some cases management lapsed before the ships were handed back to the USA, probably because the ships were out of use because of damage or other reasons.

In June 1944 *Samlamu* became the last of 182 Liberties transferred to the Red Ensign.

British records show that *Samlamu* was managed by Sir William Reardon Smith and Sons Ltd. until acquired by the Houlder Brothers' subsidiary Alexander Shipping Co. Ltd.

in April 1947. If correct, this means that this photograph of her taken In Auckland with a Houlder funnel was taken in April or May 1947 before she was named *Kingsbury*, yet she still has floats and gun tubs.

In 1960 *Kingsbury* was sold to Poland, and after serving as *Huta Bedzin*

for Polska Zegluga Morska she became a floating warehouse at Gdynia in 1969. Unromantically named *M-ZP-GDY-6* and later *MP-ZP-GDY-6*, her static role meant that she was one of the last Liberties afloat in European waters when she went to breakers at Hamina in Finland during July 1982. *[Ian J. Farquhar]*

The inspiration for the name *Samadang* came from the port city of Madang in New Guinea.

In this post-war photograph taken at Auckland managers Joseph Robinson and Sons, of Stag Line fame, have repainted her hull and funnel. A gun platform is retained on her poop and floats alongside her mainmast and it would be interesting to learn if she kept these wartime fittings after she was returned to US ownership in July 1948 and laid up in the Beaumont Reserve Fleet. Having carried just the one name, *Samadang* was broken up in New Orleans during September 1968. *[Ships in Focus]*

This US Coastguard photo shows *Sambur* on March 1944 (above), at which time there were two ships of this name on the British register. After this mistake had been discovered, she was renamed *Samwharfe* in August 1944.

On return to the United States in August 1947 she reverted to her originally intended name, *Dwight B. Heard*, and languished in the James River until taken out of lay up in 1960 and broken up at Philadelphia. *[Ian J. Farquhar]*

Naming the 182 Liberties certainly tested the creativity of British civil servants, and the inspiration behind *Samconon* is unknown. Managers B. and S. Shipping Co. Ltd. had painted up their funnel colours by the time she was photographed at Cape Town.

Samconon was returned to the USA in November 1947, and went into the Reserve Fleet at Mobile, Alabama. However, within a few months she was withdrawn and in April 1948 was sold to the Suwanee Fruit and Steamship Company of Jacksonville, Florida who put her under the Honduran flag although, unusually, they retained the name *Samconon*. In 1950 she was sold to Greek owners and the remainder of her career was spent under various flags of convenience, first as *Moderator*, then from 1955 as *Angeliki* and from 1964 as *Conchita*. On 5th July 1967 she was south west of the Seychelles during a voyage from India to Poland with ore when she developed leaks and sank. *[Ships in Focus]*

Name and	Delivery date	Maiden voyage: loading port, sailing date-intended destination	Managers	Date of end of charter new name if renamed
Adolph S Ochs		see *Samwyo*		
Ammla		see *Samvard*		
Ben H Miller	20.12.43	New York 31.1.44-Algeria	Ellerman & Papayanni Lines Ltd., Liverpool	5.6.47 *City of Shrewsbury*
Edward Bruce		see *Samoine*		
Frank A Vanderlip		see *Sambuff*		
Frederick Banting	30.12.43	New York 10.2.44-Algeria, Italy	City Line Ltd., Glasgow	19.6.47 *City of St Albans*
John J McGraw		see *Samariz*		
Samadang	29.4.44	New York 30.5.44-India	Joseph Robinson and Sons, North Shields	31.7.48
Samadre	14.4.44	New York 11.5.44-India	Hain Steamship Co. Ltd., London	11.6.47 *Maria de Larrinaga*
Samaffric	8.3.44	New York 1.4.44-Algeria, Malta	William Thomson and Co., Edinburgh	13.5.47 *Benvrackie*
Samakron	9.11.43	New York 2.12.43-India	Royal Mail Lines Ltd., London	13.9.47
Samalness	10.3.44	Baltimore 8.4.44-Egypt	Haldin and Philipps Ltd., London	10.6.47 *Castledore*
Samana	12.8.43	San Francisco 29.8.43-India	Lamport and Holt Line Ltd., Liverpool	31.7.47
Samannan	15.2.44	New York 8.3.44-Italy	Blue Star Line Ltd., London	10.7.47 *Oregon Star*
Samara	30.8.43	Baltimore 20.9.43-Egypt, Palestine renamed *Samshire* 27.9.43	Ellerman and Papayanni Lines Ltd., Liverpool	17.6.47 *City of Doncaster*
Samarina	3.9.43	Baltimore 22.9.43-Egypt	Westcott and Laurance Line Ltd., London	3.6.47 *City of Ely*
Samarinda	17.9.43	Los Angeles 29.9.43-India	T. and J. Harrison, Liverpool	13.10.47 *Student*
Samaritan	23.7.43	Iquique (Chile) 19.8.43-Egypt	Cunard White Star Ltd., Liverpool	5.6.47 *Vandalia*
Samariz	1.10.43	Baltimore 21.10.43-Egypt renamed *John J. McGraw* 3.7.44	Lamport and Holt Line Ltd., Liverpool	12.9.47 *Lassell*
Samark	8.10.43	San Francisco 16.10.43-India	Ellerman's Wilson Line Ltd., Hull	10.7.47
Samarkand	2.9.43	Philadelphia 22.9.43-Persian Gulf	Alfred Holt and Co., Liverpool	15.7.47 *Talthybius*
Samarovsk	21.8.43	Los Angeles 4.9.43-Ceylon, India	Lamport and Holt Line Ltd., Liverpool	24.7.47
Samaustral	13.5.44	Savannah (Georgia) 23.5.44-UK	J. and C. Harrison Ltd., London	24.6.47 *Harpathian*
Samavon	30.12.43	New York 22.1.44-India	Prince Line Ltd., London	5.6.47 *Pacific Nomad*
Samaye	8.9.43	Baltimore 24.9.43-Egypt	Cayzer, Irvine and Co. Ltd., London *1946:* Thomas Dunlop and Sons, Glasgow	26.6.47 *Queen Victoria*
Sambalt	18.12.43	New York 19.1.44-Persian Gulf	Cayzer, Irvine and Co. Ltd., London *1946:* David Alexander and Sons, Glasgow	28.5.47 *Lilian Moller*
Sambanka	22.4.44	New York 15.5.44-Italy	H. Hogarth and Sons, Glasgow	28.8.47
Sambay	5.8.43	Taltal (Chile) 23.9.43-Egypt	Glen Line Ltd., London	20.6.47 *Senator*
Samblade	8.8.43	Iquique (Chile) 12.9.43-Egypt	Port Line Ltd., London	28.7.47
Sambo	12.8.43	Tocopilla (Chile) 12.9.43-Egypt	Cunard White Star Ltd., Liverpool	10.11.43 (war loss)
Samboston	30.11.43	New York 22.12.43-Italy, Malta	Ellerman and Papayanni Lines Ltd., Liverpool	17.6.47 *City of Rochester*
Sambrake	20.8.43	Baltimore 13.9.43-Egypt	Ellerman and Bucknall Steam Ship Co. Ltd., London	30.5.47 *City of Chelmsford*
Sambre	9.8.43	San Francisco 27.8.43-India	Cunard White Star Ltd., Liverpool	22.8.47
Sambrian	27.8.43	Philadelphia 21.9.43-Persian Gulf	Cayzer, Irvine and Co. Ltd., London *1946:* Frank Strick and Co.Ltd., London	11.6.47 *Clan Macfarlane*
Sambridge	21.7.43	San Francisco 6.8.43-Ceylon, India	Thos. and Jno. Brocklebank Ltd., Liverpool	18.11.43 (war loss)
Sambuff	20.11.43	Baltimore 12.12.43-Egypt renamed *Frank A. Vanderlip* 18.1.44	Union-Castle Mail Steam Ship Co. Ltd., London	13.4.48
Sambur	14.9.43	Los Angeles 29.9.43-India renamed *Samwharfe* 25.8.44	Ellerman's Wilson Line Ltd., Hull	16.7.47
Samburgh	22.11.43	Baltimore 11.12.43-Egypt	Andrew Weir and Co., London	29.4.47 *Tielbank*
Sambut	21.8.43	Seattle (Washington) 6.9.43-India	P. Henderson and Co., Glasgow	6.6.44 (war loss)
Samcalia	23.9.43	Los Angeles 11.10.43-India	Furness, Withy and Co. Ltd., London	12.7.47 *Pacific Liberty*
Samcebu	10.5.44	Savannah (Georgia) 22.5.44-UK	Bolton Steam Shipping Co. Ltd., London	9.5.47 *Reynolds*
Samchess	29.1.44	New York 25.2.44-Algeria	Cayzer, Irvine and Co. Ltd., London *25.7.1946:* R.S. Dalgleish Ltd., Newcastle-on-Tyne	28.5.47 *Alpha Mooi*
Samcleve	23.11.43	Baltimore 13.12.43-Egypt	Alfred Holt and Co., Liverpool	8.11.47 *Tantalus*
Samclyde	10.1.44	New York 10.2.44-Italy	Andrew Weir and Co., London	6.6.46
Samcolne	16.3.44	New York 11.4.44-Italy	Anchor Line Ltd., Glasgow	11.6.47 *Mary Moller*
Samconon	29.2.44	New York 21.3.44-Italy	B. and S. Shipping Co. Ltd., Cardiff	7.11.47
Samconstant	26.4.44	Hampton (Virginia) 16.5.44-UK	Furness, Withy and Co. Ltd., London	21.6.47 *Skipsea*
Samcree	14.1.44	Baltimore 6.2.44-Egypt	Alfred Holt and Co., Liverpool	18.7.47
Samcrest	15.5.44	New York 10.6.44-Italy	Ellerman and Bucknall Steamship Co. Ltd., London	22.5.47 *City of Leeds*
Samdak	6.10.43	Baltimore 23.10.43-Egypt	Moss Hutchison Line Ltd., Liverpool	12.5.47 *Alpha Vaal*
Samdaring	23.3.44	New York 20.4.44-Persian Gulf	Prince Line Ltd., London	13.5.47 *Pacific Ranger*
Samdart	13.3.44	New York 10.4.44-Italy	Mungo Campbell and Co. Ltd., Newcastle-on-Tyne	23.8.47 *Sedgepool*
Samdauntless	15.4.44	Philadelphia 2.5.44-UK	William Thomson and Co., Edinburgh	28.5.47 *Bendoran*

Another naming theme borrowed from British rivers, which as in the case of *Samearn* had the attraction of brevity. Managers Houlder Brothers had certainly smartened her up by the time this photograph was taken, although gun tubs remain on the bridge wings. Houlders bought her in April 1947and gave her the name *Clarepark*, transferring her to the Claremont Shipping Co. Ltd. After just three years she went to London Greek owners as *Argolib*, remaining British registered. In 1956 New York-based owners bought her and registered her in Liberia, appropriately as *African Princess*. She was broken up in Taiwan in 1968. *[J. and M. Clarkson]*

As *Samgallion* demonstrates, Liberties quickly assumed a war-weary appearance, wartime crews having other things on their mind than keeping them neatly painted. In May 1957 *Samgallion* was sold to the Dalhousie Steam and Motor Ship Co. Ltd. of London who renamed her *Marietta Dal*, but again her career was short. On 15th May 1950 she was wrecked on the south coast of Queensland whilst on a voyage from Galveston to Brisbane and Adelaide with general cargo and sulphur. *[Ships in Focus collection]*

Samingoy was managed by the New Zealand Shipping Co. Ltd., and in June 1947 became one of two Liberties bought by their associate company within P&O, Federal Steam Navigation Co. Ltd., to become *Stafford*. Clearly stopgaps, she and her sister *Leicester* were sold in 1950 to a company based in the Bahamas but controlled from London, *Stafford* becoming *Bimini*. In 1961 a further sale saw her become *Hernan Cortes*, and with the increasingly internationalised nature of shipping her owners were nominally based in Costa Rica, her flag was Panamanian, her managers in London and her real owner in Spain. Her career was terminated by a grounding on the Yucatan Peninsula, Mexico in October 1966 and, although refloated, her 22-year-old hull was fit only for scrap. *[Ships in Focus collection]*

Samdee	17.12.43	Baltimore 21.1.44-Egypt	Thos. and Jno. Brocklebank Ltd., Liverpool	12.6.47 *Malabar*
Samdel	20.9.43	San Francisco 11.10.43-India	Ellerman's Wilson Line Ltd., Hull	4.9.47
Samderry	31.3.44	New York 20.4.44-Algeria, Italy	J. and C. Harrison Ltd., London	8.5.47 *Harpagon*
Samderwent	14.3.44	New York 1.4.44-Italy	Cayzer, Irvine and Co. Ltd., London *1946:* Frank Strick and Co. Ltd., London	11.6.47 *Clan Macfadyen*
Samdon	31.12.43	New York 22.1.44-Algeria, Italy	Cayzer, Irvine and Co. Ltd., London	12.2.46
Samdonard	29.3.44	New York 21.4.44-Algeria	McCowen and Gross Ltd., London	29.7.47 *Daybeam*
Samearn	31.1.44	New York 18.2.44-Italy	Houlder Line Ltd., London	25.4.47 *Clarepark*
Sameden	14.3.44	New York 11.4.44-Italy	Port Line Ltd., London	4.6.47 *Mill Hill*
Samesk	5.2.44	Baltimore 1.3.44-Egypt	New Zealand Shipping Co. Ltd., London	29.4.47 *Leicester*
Samettrick	12.1.44	New York 20.2.44-Algeria, Italy	P. & O. Steam Navigation Co., London	23.5.47 *Elstree Grange*
Sameveron	17.1.44	New York 10.2.44-Algeria, Italy There is evidence that she was originally named *Samjack.*	Orient Steam Navigation Co. Ltd., London *1946:* Trinder, Anderson and Co., London	7.8.47 *Ericbank*
Samfairy	28.3.44	New York 19.4.44-Egypt	Haldin and Philipps, London	1.8.47 *Admiral Cunningham*
Samfaithful	9.5.44	New York 30.5.44-Italy	Royal Mail Lines Ltd., London	25.6.47 *Balantia*
Samfeugh	19.1.44	Baltimore 9.2.44-Egypt	Charles Hill and Sons, Bristol	4.9.47
Samfield	29.11.43	New York 23.12.43-Italy	Cayzer, Irvine and Co. Ltd., London *1946:* Walter Runciman and Co. Ltd., Newcastle-on-Tyne	15.5.47 *Southmoor*
Samfinn	13.4.44	New York 9.5.44-UK	Donaldson Brothers and Black Ltd., Glasgow	9.9.47
Samfleet	6.5.44	New York 30.5.44-Egypt	Andrew Weir and Co., London	24.5.47 *Corabank*
Samflora	17.11.43	Baltimore 1.12.43-Egypt	Union-Castle Mail Steam Ship Co. Ltd., London	29.8.47 *Primrose Hill*
Samforth	6.1.44	New York 1.2.44-Central Med	Alfred Holt and Co., Liverpool	13.7.48
Samfoyle	31.3.44	Boston 7.5.44-UK	Cunard White Star Ltd., Liverpool	27.5.47 *Vardulia*
Samfreedom	23.5.44	New York 9.6.44-Persian Gulf	Counties Ship Management Co. Ltd., London	24.4.47 *Finnamore Hill*
Samgallion	31.3.44	New York 21.4.44-Italy	E.J. Sutton and Co., Newcastle-on-Tyne	2.5.47 *Marietta Dal*
Samgara	25.11.43	Baltimore 13.12.43-Egypt	Alfred Holt and Co., Liverpool	23.5.47 *Titan*
Samgaudie	8.3.44	Philadelphia 30.3.44-India	Thos. and Jno. Brocklebank Ltd., Liverpool	18.7.47 *Norah Moller*
Samglory	29.4.44	Baltimore 15.5.44-Egypt	Dodd, Thomson and Co. Ltd., London	10.9.47 *Serbistan*
Samhain	23.8.43	Baltimore 10.9.43-Egypt	Ellerman and Bucknall Steam Ship Co. Ltd., London	7.5.47 *City of Portsmouth*
Samharle	23.12.43	New York 29.1.44-Algeria	Alfred Holt and Co., Liverpool	4.6.47 *Troilus*
Samholt	17.7.43	Los Angeles 31.7.43-India	Cunard White Star Ltd., Liverpool	30.7.47
Samhope	5.4.44	New York 29.4.44-Italy	Sir William Reardon Smith and Sons Ltd., Cardiff	18.7.47 *Rosalie Moller*
Samhorn	23.2.44	Baltimore 1.4.44-Egypt	Donaldson Brothers and Black, Ltd., Glasgow	8.5.48
Samida	25.9.43	Los Angeles 9.10.43-India	P. & O. Steam Navigation Co., London	10.4.45 (war loss)
Samidway	17.5.44	Portland (Maine) 25.5.44-UK	Alfred Holt and Co., Liverpool	8.7.47 *Scholar*
Samindoro	17.6.44	New York 2.7.44-Italy	Headlam and Son, Whitby	18.6.47 *Sandsend*
Samingoy	13.5.44	Baltimore 8.6.44-Egypt	New Zealand Shipping Co. Ltd., London	24.6.47 *Stafford*
Saminver	22.2.44	Baltimore 16.3.44-UK	Blue Star Line Ltd., London	6.5.48
Samite	26.8.43	Baltimore 12.9.43-Egypt	Alfred Holt and Co., Liverpool	30.9.47
Samjack	27.3.44	New York 30.4.44-India	Alfred Holt and Co., Liverpool	25.7.47 *Tydeus*
Samkansa	4.10.43	Baltimore 23.10.43-Egypt	Orient Steam Navigation Co. Ltd., London *1946:* General Steam Navigation Co.,London	5.6.47 *Cerinthus*
Samkey	24.12.43	New York 3.2.44-Italy	New Zealand Shipping Co. Ltd., London	31.1.48 (marine loss)

Nikola Tesla was launched on 25th September 1943, but when delivered in a remarkable time of just nine days she had become *Samkansa*, another name inspired by an American state. She was one of relatively few British-operated Liberties which switched managers, General Steam taking over from Orient Steam Navigation in 1946, and no doubt the coaster company found they were running a ship much bigger than anything they had done previously. On sale in June 1947 she became *Cerinthus* of Hadley Shipping Co. Ltd. under Houlder management. From 1952 she had a succession of London-Greek owners, first as

Phassa and from 1953 as *Urania*, going to Hong Kong owners as *Concord Venture* in 1964, and ending her days with Japanese breakers in early 1970. *Samkansa* was photographed by the US Coastguard on 4th April 1944. *[Ian J. Farquhar collection]*

Once peace came, managers quickly painted up their own funnel colours, as did Moss Hutchison Line Ltd. with *Samlyth*. In October 1947 she became *St. Arvans* of South American Saint Line, continuing with this Cardiff owner until sold to Sovtorgflot as *Sajany* in 1963. She was broken up at Split, Yugoslavia in April 1972. *[Ships in Focus collection]*

Samlamu	26.6.44	Baltimore 12.7.44-India	Sir William Reardon Smith and Sons Ltd., Cardiff	1.5.47 *Kingsbury*
Samlea	22.3.44	New York 20.4.44-India	Ellerman and Bucknall Steamship Co. Ltd., London	15.5.47 *City of Colchester*
Samleven	14.2.44	New York 11.3.44-Italy	Port Line Ltd., London	29.7.47 *Bisham Hill*
Samleyte	1.5.44	Baltimore 21.5.44-Egypt	C.T. Bowring and Co. Ltd., London	5.9.47
Samlistar	31.5.44	Baltimore 20.6.44-India	Mungo Campbell and Co. Ltd., Newcastle-on-Tyne	2.6.47 *Hurworth*
Samlong	17.11.43	Philadelphia 2.12.43-India	Prince Line Ltd., London	29.1.49
Samlorian	20.5.44	Savannah (Georgia) 13.6.44-UK	E.R. Management Co. Ltd., Cardiff	10.7.47 *Helmspey*
Samlossie	22.2.44	New York 10.4.44-India	P. Henderson and Co., Glasgow	10.7.47 *Barn Hill*
Samlouis	5.11.43	Philadelphia 30.11.43-India	Ellerman's Wilson Line Ltd., Hull	28.4.47 *Coralstone*
Samloyal	29.4.44	Baltimore 16.5.44-UK	B. and S. Shipping Co. Ltd., Cardiff	7.5.47 *St Helena*
Samluzon	12.6.44	New York 2.7.44-Italy	Morel Ltd., Cardiff	30.6.47 *Jersey May*
Samlyth	21.2.44	Baltimore 11.3.44-Egypt	Moss Hutchison Line Ltd., Liverpool	7.10.47 *St Arvans*
Sammex	5.10.43	Baltimore 19.10.43-Egypt	General Steam Navigation Co. Ltd., London	5.6.47 *Sheaf Mead*
Sammont	30.9.43	Los Angeles 15.10.43-India	William Thomson and Co., Edinburgh	23.9.47 *Salmonier*
Samneagh	6.4.44	Portland (Maine) 2.5.44-UK	P. Henderson and Co., Glasgow	28.5.47 *Stamford Hill*
Samnebra	18.10.43	Baltimore 4.11.43-Egypt	Cayzer, Irvine and Co. Ltd., London *30.4.1946:* Chellew Navigation Co. Ltd., Cardiff	22.8.47 *Pentire*
Samnegros	22.6.44	New York 21.7.44-Italy	G. Nisbet and Co., Glasgow	30.10.47 *Titanbank*
Samnesse	18.10.43	Philadelphia 9.11.43-India	Alfred Holt and Co., Liverpool	19.5.47 *Eumaeus*
Samnethy	10.3.44	New York 1.4.44-Italy	E.R. Management Co. Ltd., Cardiff	13.5.48

Samnegros was another name inspired by a Pacific location, this time part of the Philippines. Photographed by John McRoberts in the Mersey, she retains her floats and gun tubs but has been painted in the colours of her managers, G. Nisbet and Co. of Glasgow. She too went to Bank Line in 1947 as *Titanbank*, and from 1959 had a string of Far Eastern owners, becoming successively *Lucina*, *Candy*, and *Yvonne* before being scrapped in Taiwan in 1967. *[John McRoberts/Roy Fenton collection]*

Edward J. Bruce briefly carried the name *Samoine* but, her being named after an associate of President Roosevelt, pressure was applied to restore her original name. Returned to the US in July 1947, she went into lay up in the James River and remained there until broken up at Kearny, New Jersey in 1971. She and many other Liberties, which cost well in excess of a million dollars to build, thus spent just four years in service.

The wartime photograph shows her with long poles on two of her masts for handling torpedo nets. *[Ships in Focus collection]*

Samneva	27.9.43	Los Angeles 12.10.43-Ceylon, India	Alfred Holt and Co., Liverpool	2.8.47
Samnid	24.1.44	Baltimore 10.2.44-Egypt	Blue Star Line Ltd., London	2.7.47 *Pacific Star*
Samoa	23.8.43	New York 12.9.43-Persian Gulf	Alfred Holt and Co., Liverpool	29.4.47 *Eurymedon*
Samoine	15.11.43	Baltimore 1.12.43-Egypt renamed *Edward Bruce* 11.1.44	Stanley and John Thompson Ltd., London	22.7.47
Samois	8.11.43	Baltimore 23.11.43-Egypt	Westcott and Laurance Line Ltd., London	19.6.47 *City of Lichfield*
Samokla	3.11.43	New York 2.12.43-India 30.4.1946: Dene Shipping Co. Ltd., London	Cayzer, Irvine and Co. Ltd., London	19.4.48
Samoland	9.6.44	New York 1.7.44-Algeria	Watts, Watts and Co. Ltd., London	28.6.47 *Sea Triumph*
Samora	7.9.43	Baltimore 22.9.43-Egypt renamed *Sampenn* 5.11.44 30.4.1946: Charles Strubin and Co. Ltd., London	Cayzer, Irvine and Co. Ltd., London	24.8.48
Samoresby	29.4.44	New York 29.5.44-India	B. and S. Shipping Co. Ltd., Cardiff 1947: Mungo Campbell and Co. Ltd., Newcastle-on-Tyne	16.4.48
Samos	30.8.43	Baltimore 18.9.43-Egypt	Elder Dempster Lines Ltd., Liverpool	3.5.47 *Zini*
Samota	13.10.43	Baltimore 30.10.43-Egypt	Elder Dempster Lines Ltd., Liverpool	5.5.47 *Zungeru*
Samothrace	11.9.43	Baltimore 29.9.43-Egypt	Pacific Steam Navigation Co., Liverpool	22.5.47 *Talca*
Samouri	2.10.43	Seattle (Washington) 15.10.43 -India	Moss Hutchison Line Ltd., Liverpool	26.1.44 (war loss)
Samouse	26.1.44	New York 19.2.44-Italy	Cunard White Star Ltd., Liverpool	21.5.47 *Marabank*
Samovar	30.7.43	San Francisco 20.8.43-Egypt	Thos. and Jno. Brocklebank Ltd., Liverpool	14.6.47 *Kansi*
Sampa	6.9.43	Baltimore 23.9.43-Egypt	Houlder Brothers and Co. Ltd., London	27.2.45 (war loss)
Sampan	17.8.43	Los Angeles 30.8.43-India	Union-Castle Mail Steamship Co., London	28.10.47
Sampenn		see *Samora*		
Sampep	1.9.43	Los Angeles 12.9.43-India	Houlder Brothers and Co. Ltd., London	24.5.48
Sampford	12.9.43	San Francisco 1.10.43-India	Andrew Weir and Co., London	25.4.47 *Rowanbank*
Samphill	9.11.43	Philadelphia 2.12.43-India	Royal Mail Lines Ltd., London	5.5.47 *Berbice*
Samphire	22.8.43	Baltimore 22.9.43-Egypt	P. Henderson and Co., Glasgow	1.10.47
Sampler	21.7.43	Seattle (Washington) 8.8.43-India	Port Line Ltd., London	9.5.47 *Port Albany*
Samport	14.12.43	Baltimore 2.1.44-Egypt	Cayzer, Irvine and Co. Ltd., London 1946: Maclay, McIntyre Ltd., Glasgow	28.4.48
Samrich	20.11.43	New York 12.12.43-India	Shaw Savill and Albion Co. Ltd., London	21.5.47 *Cufic*

On *Sampler* was bestowed one of the few 'real' names given to the Liberties, although hardly one to stir the imagination. Here she appears to be in the colours of Port Line Ltd., who bought her in May 1947 and renamed her *Port Albany*. Sold in 1953, London-Greeks first named her *Teni* then *Gloriana*. She was broken up at Shanghai in 1968. *[Ships in Focus collection]*

Samrich had already assumed Shaw, Savill livery when photographed at Cape Town, and later became their *Cufic*. Further names carried were *Santa Elisabetta* in 1953 for Italian owners and *Star* in 1967 for London-Greeks. Taiwan breakers dismantled her in 1968. *[Ships in Focus]*

Samsacola	29.12.43	Philadelphia 2.2.44-India	Stanley and John Thompson Ltd., London	28.8.47 *Silvercedar*
Samselbu	26.4.44	Savannah (Georgia) 14.5.44-UK	Walter Runciman and Co. Ltd., Newcastle-on-Tyne	19.3.45 (war loss)
Samsette	12.11.43	Baltimore 27.11.43-Egypt	Alfred Holt and Co., Liverpool	15.7.47 *Eurypylus*
Samshee	21.3.44	Philadelphia 6.4.44-India	Hain Steamship Co. Ltd., London	16.6.48
			7.1946: W.H. Seager and Co. Ltd., Newcastle-on-Tyne	
Samshire		see *Samara*		
Samsip	9.11.43	New York 12.12.43-Ceylon, India	New Zealand Shipping Co. Ltd., London	7.12.44 (war loss)
Samskern	15.6.44	New York 2.7.44-Italy	Evan Thomas Radcliffe and Co., Cardiff	27.6.47 *Stanthorpe*
Samsmola	25.5.44	New York 10.6.44-India	Ellerman's Wilson Line Ltd., Hull.	10.12.47
Samsoaring	29.5.44	New York 21.6.44-Italy	P. & O. Steam Navigation Co., London	25.9.47 *Fraser River*
Samson	21.7.43	Los Angeles 3.8.43-India	Cunard White Star Ltd., Liverpool	22.6.48
Samspeed	3.6.44	New York 21.6.44-India	Lyle Shipping Co. Ltd., Glasgow	30.6.47 *Cape York*
Samspelga	25.3.44	New York 19.4.44-Persian Gulf	John Morrison and Son, Newcastle-on-Tyne	30.10.47 *Springbank*
Samsperrin	18.3.44	New York 11.4.44-Italy	Hain Steamship Co. Ltd., London	4.10.47
Samspring	16.12.43	New York 11.1.44-Algeria, Italy	Royal Mail Lines Ltd., London	28.4.47 *Beresina*
Samsteel	15.8.43	Los Angeles 29.8.43-India	Union-Castle Mail Steam Ship Co. Ltd., London	9.9.47
Samstrae	27.2.44	New York 21.3.44-Italy	Headlam and Son, Whitby	7.7.47 *Sneaton*
Samstrule	16.2.44	New York 11.3.44-Italy	Elders and Fyffes Ltd., London	20.5.47 *Artemisia*
Samsturdy	12.4.44	Baltimore 3.5.44-UK	Common Brothers Ltd., Newcastle-on-Tyne	6.5.47 *Baluchistan*
Samsurf	5.8.43	Los Angeles 16.8.43-India	Cunard White Star Ltd., Liverpool	24.5.48
Samsuva	13.5.44	Portland (Maine) 22.5.44-UK	Sir Robert Ropner and Co. Ltd., West Hartlepool	29.9.44 (war loss)
Samsylarna	24.6.44	New York 12.7.44-India	Sir Robert Ropner and Co. Ltd., West Hartlepool	8.2.49
Samsylvan	27.10.43	Baltimore 13.11.43-Egypt	Shaw Savill and Albion Co. Ltd., London	17.6.47 *Tropic*
Samtampa	22.12.43	New York 22.1.44-Italy	Houlder Line Ltd., London	23.4.47 (marine loss)
Samtana	9.6.44	Baltimore 25.6.44-India	Lyle Shipping Co. Ltd., Glasgow	4.6.47 *Cape Verde*
Samtay	20.1.44	New York 20.2.44-Egypt	Blue Star Line Ltd., London	10.10.47 *Rudby*
Samteviot	8.2.44	New York 2.3.44-Italy	Trinder, Anderson and Co., London	23.7.47
Samthar	5.9.43	Vancouver 25.9.43-Ceylon, India	Royal Mail Lines Ltd., London	19.5.47 *Barranca*
Samtorch	31.5.44	Baltimore 21.6.44-India	Ellerman and Papayanni Lines Ltd., Liverpool	6.6.47 *City of Stafford*
Samtredy	21.9.43	Los Angeles 4.10.43-India	Prince Line Ltd., London	7.8.47 *Pacific Importer*
Samtrent	30.11.43	New York 12.12.43-India	Union-Castle Mail Steam Ship Co. Ltd., London	13.10.47
Samtroy	7.12.43	New York 11.1.44-Italy, Malta	Andrew Weir and Co., London	13.6.47 *Edenbank*
Samtrusty	22.4.44	New York 19.5.44-India	Donaldson Brothers and Black Ltd., Glasgow	22.5.47 *Lakonia*
Samtruth	25.5.44	New York 10.6.44-Egypt	Haldin and Philipps Ltd., London	6.2.48
Samtucky	30.10.43	Philadelphia 22.11.43-India	Prince Line Ltd., London	4.6.48
Samtweed	30.12.43	New York 31.1.44-Italy	Hall Line Ltd., Liverpool	26.6.47 *City of Newport*
Samtyne	24.2.44	New York 11.3.44-Italy	Royal Mail Lines Ltd., London	18.6.47 *Argentine Transport*
Samur	1.9.43	Baltimore 20.9.43-Egypt	Lamport and Holt Line Ltd., Liverpool	13.5.48
Samuta	12.11.43	Baltimore 22.11.43-Egypt	Andrew Weir and Co., London	1.7.47 *Kelvinbank*
Samvannah	30.12.43	Baltimore 2.2.44-Egypt	Anchor Line Ltd., Glasgow	13.5.48
Samvard	13.12.43	New York 1.1.44-Egypt renamed *Ammla* 8.2.44	William Thomson and Co., Edinburgh	4.7.47 *Benarty*
Samvern	28.10.43	New York 19.11.43-Persian Gulf	William Thomson and Co., Leith	18.1.45 (war loss)

The pattern of wear on the paintwork of *Samstrae* at Auckland suggest it was largely a result of handling cargo overside, probably into lighters or landing craft. Managers Headlam and Son bought her in July 1947 and as *Sneaton* she spent the rest of her career with this Whitby firm. When she arrived at Taiwan for breaking in July 1967 she was the second to last Liberty in mainland British ownership, the very last being her sister in the Headlam fleet, *Sandsend* ex-*Samindoro*. [Ian J. Farquhar]

Samvigna	20.4.44	New York 20.5.44-Ceylon	Hain Steamship Co. Ltd., London	30.6.48
Samwake	28.4.44	Boston 25.5.44-UK	Stanley and John Thompson Ltd., London	31.7.44 (war loss)
Samwash	13.9.43	San Francisco 2.10.43-India	Andrew Weir and Co., London	3.5.47 *Maplebank*
Samwater	16.8.43	Baltimore 3.9.43-Egypt	Glen Line Ltd., London	29.1.47 (marine loss)
Samwharfe		see *Sambur*		
Samwinged	30.4.44	New York 19.5.44-UK	Sir William Reardon Smith and Sons Ltd., Cardiff	5.6.48
Samwis	15.10.43	Philadelphia 10.11.43-India	T. and J. Harrison, Liverpool	20.6.47 *Specialist*
Samwye	8.3.44	New York 31.3.44-Italy	Andrew Weir and Co., London	10.6.47 *Willowbank*
Samwyo	2.10.43	Baltimore 21.10.43-Egypt renamed *Adolph S. Ochs* 20.12.43	Cayzer, Irvine and Co. Ltd., London *30.4.1946:* George Nisbet and Co., Glasgow	25.6.48
Samyale	17.12.43	Baltimore 11.1.44-Egypt	Booth Steam Ship Co. Ltd., Liverpool	26.8.47 *Zungon*
Samyork	29.10.43	New York 22.11.43-India	Andrew Weir and Co., London	10.6.47 *Ivybank*
Samythian	21.1.44	New York 18.2.44-Italy	Kaye, Son and Co. Ltd., London	28.10.47
Samzona	19.9.43	Tacoma (Washington) 4.10.43 -India	Royal Mail Lines Ltd., London	8.5.48

To be continued

In contrast to most other ships illustrated here, *Samvannah* looks almost pristine and has obviously just been completed. The poles for torpedo nets are clearly visible, as are the lengthened cross trees for securing them, and she appears fully armed. The white-painted funnel and upper masts were presumably an attempt to reduce their visibility. *Samvannah* was a late return to the USA, in May 1948, and her original name *Louis A. Godey* was restored, a fairly pointless exercise as she then languished in the Beaumont Reserve Fleet until taken out in March 1961 and broken up at Orange, Texas. [Ships in Focus collection]

113

RECORD BOOKS
LIBERTY SHIPS
Roy Fenton

The publication of the first part of John de Winser's article on Liberties on charter to Britain offers an excuse to look back at the five major works on this type of ship. Not considered, because of their narrow remit, are those that concern the Liberty ships transferred to the Greek and French flags after the Second World War.

The first book to provide a complete and detailed listing of these ships was 'The Liberty Ships' by L.A. Sawyer and W.H. Mitchell, first published in 1970 with a second edition by Lloyd's of London Press in 1985. Much more than a catalogue, it goes into some depth on the background to the building of the Liberties, including their adaptation from the design of J.L. Thompson and Sons' *Empire Liberty*. Also well covered are details of construction and equipment, war losses, post-war disposals, conversions both military and civilian, the 'Sam' ships, the reserve fleet and the preserved *Jeremiah O'Brien*. The products of each yard are listed, with month and date of completion, engine builder, all subsequent names with dates, and brief details of fates. The ship biographies are rather short (owners are not listed), but major incidents and other significant events merit additional paragraphs. Photographs are sparse but, immaculately researched and carefully written, Sawyer and Mitchell's book was not only groundbreaking but has yet to be surpassed.

Next in chronological order came Ian Stewart's 'Liberty Ships in Peacetime', published by the Australian author in 1992. His introductory sections cover much of the same ground as Mitchell and Sawyer, and then he gives a detailed, year-by-year account of the commercial role of Liberties post-war. The meat of the book consists of career details of every Liberty that saw commercial service after the war. The information goes beyond that given by Sawyer and Mitchell in listing all owners' names, and – very welcome to your reviewer – includes many of the Greek and other operators who lay behind the often anonymously named flag-of-convenience companies. There are also more details of losses and demolitions. The author was very keen on giving the buyer value for money in terms of using every square inch of paper, and the book is very thoroughly illustrated. There are indexes, cross references, tables, and appendices galore, but the sources and acknowledgements listed have one bizarre omission: Sawyer and Mitchell's book.

Although it might have appeared that previous authors had written the last word on Liberties, Peter Elphick proved this wrong in 2001. Apart from its clichéd title, his 'Liberty: the Ships that Won the War' is an excellent book, its three sections dealing in considerable detail with the development and building of the ships, their wartime service and peacetime roles, the last-named section being relatively short and selective. Elphick's research, for the first part especially, is exemplary. For instance he has searched out the surviving members of the British Shipbuilding Mission who played a key role in the design of the Liberties (whatever anyone in the USA might think). With over 400 informants, and his detailed research in archives around the world, Elphick has written a highly accessible and dependable account, and dispelled several myths about the Liberties. His book does not contain details of individual ships, and its photographic content is no more than adequate (at least in the paperback edition published by Chatham in 2006), but it is an excellent complement to Sawyer and Mitchell's work. .

In 2004 came what is undoubtedly the heaviest book on the subject and the most unwieldy title: 'The Liberty Ships from A (A.B. Hammond) to Z (Zona Gale)' by Walter W. Jaffe (Glencannon, Palo Alto, 2004). The ships are listed in several rather arbitrary sections: those lost in wartime, those which ended up in the reserve fleet, those which sailed commercially post war, foreign-government owned ships, and those sunk as artificial fish reefs. The author presents some data not previously published, including the origin of each ship's name, the dates of its keel laying, launch and delivery, and its wartime operator. There is considerable detail concerning the circumstances of losses, and when and where ships entered reserve fleets, but for the Liberties which served commercially the details of ownership and breakers are less complete than those in Ian Stewart's book. Photographs are far fewer too (with the honourable exception of some excellent shots of yards and construction), and reproduction suggests some were taken from newspapers or magazines. It is unlikely that the listing of US operators is complete: only one operator is given for each ship, but several Liberties were reactivated having once gone into reserve, and would surely have had new operators. What really lets this by no-means inexpensive book down is the text. Hoary myths are perpetuated, including that the 'Sam' names given by the British Ministry of War Transport were a reference to the generosity of 'Uncle Sam' (repeated 182 times), and one exploded by Elphick that the design taken to the USA by the British Shipbuilding Mission dated from 1879. England is confused with Britain, and the 'Ocean' class are described as 'Liberties'. The role of the British Shipbuilding Mission is underplayed, and it seems the author has not really understood the phenomenon of brittle fracture which led to welded hulls of several Liberties and other ships cracking. He has not read, or perhaps not absorbed, what his predecessors have written, and such errors make one suspicious of other information he includes. It is ironic that the most disappointing book on these United States-built ships was written by a US citizen.

The most reliable source of career data for the Liberties is the 'Register of Merchant Ships Completed in the U.S.A. 1942-1945 Part III – Liberty Ships' compiled by Wm. A. Schell. Produced in two parts, this is in the series of Starke-Schell Registers published by the World Ship Society. In common with the others in the series, this lists all subsequent names and owners (including those behind the flag-of-convenience operations) and concise but intensively researched details of fates. The series format is to list hull but not engine builders, and users should be aware that the port listed following the owners' details is that of registration, not of domicile.

Deservedly for such a huge and important fleet of ships, the Liberties have been better researched and written about than almost any other group of cargo ships. However, no single work has all the information that an interested reader would want about the ships, singularly or collectively, excuse – if one is needed – for adding them all to one's library.

SHELL'S FORMER SAILING SHIP TANKERS
Malcolm Cooper

The combination of heavy wartime losses, the dislocation of shipbuilding resources and the disruption of normal trading practices by port congestion and government requisitions during the First World War produced acute tonnage shortages across the British shipping industry. This was a particular problem in the tanker sector. Here the general problems were accentuated by the disproportionate impact of losses on a relatively small and specialised fleet. In addition, the war itself had accelerated the replacement of coal by oil, not least in the Royal Navy's most modern ships, and increased demand in its turn had broadened the already global reach of the oil industry and its transportation network.

Even before the war ended, both the government and private sector oil companies were casting around for solutions to the tanker shortage. New building would take time, not least because yard space itself was at a premium. One solution was the adoption of war standard ships to bulk oil carriage, a programme which produced the AO and Z type classes - ordered as dry cargo vessels but with tanks built into their hull space. Another, more exotic expedient was to convert sailing vessels to steam or motor tankers.

The genesis of the conversion programme
The idea was the brainchild of Cornelius Zulver, the Marine Superintendent of the oil company Shell. Zulver sought to produce much-needed tanker tonnage by fitting diesel engines originally produced for submarines but now surplus to Admiralty requirements into the hulls of otherwise redundant sailing ships. On the face of things, this might have seemed a needlessly complicated procedure, but a number of factors, apart from the availability of the engines themselves, weighed in its favour. The first was simply that there were a number of sailing vessels available – ships with little obvious commercial future, whose conversion would not make inroads into dry cargo carrying capacity, and whose owners were likely to be only too willing to sell at prices well above their peacetime break-up value. The second was that conversion itself was more straightforward than might first have seemed the case. The great advantage of a sailing ship hull was that it was basically an empty shell into which tank storage could be fitted, encumbered neither by hold bulkheads nor midship machinery space. The partial removal of masts and rigging was a fairly quick process, as was the construction of a basic superstructure. It should also have been fairly straightforward to retro-fit engines into the after part of an otherwise empty hull. The size of the hulls and consequent dependence on compact propulsion machinery would mean that the resulting tankers were likely to be neither fit nor economical for long-distance work. They could, however, fill the need for coastal tank tonnage to employ in distant waters.

In 1917-1919, the Anglo-Saxon Petroleum Co. Ltd. acquired a total of eight sailing vessels for conversion to twin-screw steam or motor tankers. Shell was acting with the full support of the government's Shipping Controller. Indeed, the conversion programme appears to have been supported by active government intervention. In three cases, the Shipping Controller acted as the initial purchasing agent for the acquisition of the vessels and only sold them on to Shell at a later date, either during or after conversion itself. In at least one case the Controller appears effectively to have forced an unwilling sailing ship owner to sell.

The ships themselves had all been built by British shipyards between 1891 and 1902, a period which witnessed the final flourish of investment in new sail tonnage. Five were products of the minor sail construction boom of the early 1890s; and one was a member of the fairly small group of British vessels built after 1895 when the boom had just about run its course. The last two had been built by Archibald McMillan of Dumbarton for foreign owners in 1902. The one other builder to contribute two vessels was Workman Clark of Belfast, building to the order of two separate Irish owners.

Most of the ships had fairly tangled or even exotic histories. Every vessel had long since been sold by its original owner, largely as a result of the mass exodus of British ship owners from a sailing trade squeezed by falling profits and increasing insurance costs. In several cases the war itself had added further twists to the ownership record. After conversion, the ships were all eventually given a name ending with *Shell*, and in each case the new owner managed to find a name starting with the same letter as that carried by the sailing ship at the time of its acquisition!

While the vessels were UK-owned at the time of purchase, and all were ultimately registered in London, acquisition and conversion were both global in scope. Many of the sailing vessels were in far-flung foreign ports when ownership changed. With some of the conversions taking place in the Far East, roughly half the fleet never saw a UK port during their tanker careers. In addition, the re-building programme was very drawn out. While the first acquisitions were converted very quickly, the momentum appears to have gone out of the programme with the return of peace. By the time the last of the group emerged in its new guise, some of its earlier peers had already departed the scene by one means or another.

Wartime acquisitions
The first vessel acquired for the conversion programme was easily the smallest. Built for their own account by the Bristol shipbuilders and owners Charles Hill and Sons in 1891, this modest-sized three-masted barque had served three owners under her original, rather prosaic name of *Gladys*. She had spent the bulk of her career with Shaw, Savill and Co., but was finally sold to Shell in July 1917 by the more obscure TalTal Shipping Co. Ltd. At the time she was laying at the South African port of Knysna and, with no qualified master available, she was sailed east to Hong Kong for conversion under the command of an officer holding only a first mate's certificate. The rebuilding process appears to have been fairly basic. The masts were left intact, the rig simply being reduced from barque to barquentine, only the most basic

The barque *Gladys* would seem an unlikely candidate for conversion to a tanker. With her unbroken sheerline, raised quarterdeck and single topgallants, she more closely resembled the small but elegant iron vessels of the 1870s and 1880s than the big steel carriers of the decade in which she was built. *[John Naylon collection]*

superstructure was added, and the cylinder heads of the 1915-built Swedish pair of four-cylinder diesels were left protruding above deck level. The vessel was renamed *Gaper Shell* in January 1918, conversion was completed a month later, and she was formally re-registered as a twin-screw motor tanker in May. Her subsequent career was brief, as she ran aground on passage between Singapore and Beira on 25th January 1919 and broke up four days later.

Shell's second acquisition took place a few days after the first. Once again the vessel was a three-masted barque, although both larger and newer than the *Gladys*. Like this vessel she had already served three owners, but in this case under three different names with three different ports of registry. Built in 1897 as the London-registered *Haytor*, she was sold after little more than a year to the short-lived Dundee fleet of Robert Ferguson and renamed *Earnmount* (Ferguson's ships were all given names ending in – *mount*, his most notable vessel being the *Islamount*, now restored as a Clyde museum ship under her original name *Glenlee*). Ferguson's small fleet was sold off around 1905 and *Earnmount* went to the established Liverpool-Welsh company of Robert Thomas and Co, who renamed her *Dolbadarn Castle*. Following acquisition for £31,500, she received another fairly basic conversion at Hong Kong. All three of her masts were converted to schooner rig, she was fitted with a rudimentary bridge amidships, and once again the cylinder heads of her twin diesels (an identical pair to those fitted in the *Gaper Shell*) were left above deck. She was renamed *Dolphin Shell* on the same day as her predecessor changed names, with conversion being complete by March 1918. She would remain in service, entirely in the East, until 1931.

The next two acquisitions in December 1917 and February 1918 were typical examples of the large four-masted barques produced in some quantity by British ship-builders in the early 1890s. *Celticburn* and *Howth* had been launched within two months of each other, the first for Shankland's Greenock-based Burn Line, and the second for Sir Robert Martin of Dublin. Both had changed owners, in the second case several times, but both were still carrying their original names when Shell stepped in. The *Celticburn* was not re-registered as the twin-screw motor tanker *Circe Shell* until April 1919 and did not leave UK waters for the Far East until early 1920. The *Howth* was actually at New York when she was purchased, but although she was quickly renamed *Horn Shell*, she actually sailed to Australia before proceeding to Hong Kong for conversion, with re-registration taking place in October 1919. Both vessels emerged rigged as four-masted schooners, sporting identical pairs of new eight-cylinder Vickers diesels – this time located entirely below deck. Neither ship enjoyed a very long second career in Far Eastern waters, with both leaving the fleet by the end of 1925.

Shell's last direct acquisition was the largest former sailing ship to enter the fleet and the only one to be fitted with steam engines rather than diesels. She could also lay claim to one of the most unusual past histories. Built in 1902 at Dumbarton as *Urania* for B. Wencke Sohne of Hamburg, she was one of only a handful of German sailing ships built outside Germany after the 1890s. Having been sold along with the rest of her fleet mates to another Hamburg firm in 1906, she was captured at sea by the Royal Navy in 1914 while sailing homewards ignorant of the declaration of war. Condemned as a prize, she was sold to R. Brailli and Company of Cardiff and registered at London with the unusual (and rather optimistic) name of *Speedonia*. Brailli formed the single-ship company Speedonia Ltd. to own his new acquisition. This company had a registered capital of only £2,000, suggesting that the Admiralty was more interested in getting rid of the vessel than in realising her

CELTICBURN.

The heavily-rigged *Celticburn* was one of six baldheaders built by Barclay, Curle for Shankland's Burn Line. *[John Naylon collection]*

true market worth. Shell purchased her in June 1918, but she continued to operate as a sailing vessel under her original name until 1921. In that year she was at last renamed *Scala Shell* and taken in hand for conversion in the UK, emerging in her new guise as a twin-screw steam tanker in early 1922. She sailed for the Far East looking far less like a one-time sailing vessel than most of the fleet. Two of her masts were cut away entirely, and the yards were removed from the other two, making room for some normal tanker superstructure, including a substantial bridge/accommodation block amidships. Because of the significant delay between acquisition and conversion, the *Scala Shell* entered service after all seven of her diesel-powered compatriots.

Peacetime acquisitions from the Shipping Controller
The last three vessels of the Shell programme were all purchased from the Shipping Controller on 8th September 1919, more than a year after the company's direct acquisitions from the commercial market had ceased. In all three cases, conversion appears at least to have begun before the vessel changed hands and, as Shell had been appointed manager at the time of the original government acquisition, it seems likely that the vessels had been intended for the Shell tanker fleet all along.

The three were all large four-masted barques, but they had distinctly different pasts. The 1892-built *Goodrich* had spent only three years with her original owners before becoming the Russian-flagged but Finnish-owned *Fennia*.

She was still Finnish-owned when acquired by the British government, although the exact date of this acquisition is not clear as the Shipping Controller did not bother to re-enter her in the British register until July 1919, after conversion to a motor tanker. Conversion was completed under government auspices and Shell did not purchase the vessel until six weeks after registration. The *Fennia* received identical twin eight-cylinder Vickers diesels to the *Circe Shell* and *Horn Shell*, but was given a far more drastic structural overhaul, losing all but one of her masts in the process. She differed from all five of the direct Shell acquisitions in being sent to the Mediterranean rather than the Far East. For some reason official sanction to change the names of all three of the vessels acquired from the Shipping Controller was not granted until 14th December 1920, and the name on the ship's register papers was not altered from *Fennia* to *Fionashell* until March 1921 when the vessel was laying at Suez.

The second of the trio acquired via the Shipping Controller was the *Oweenee* of 1891. She was British-built, but one of only a handful of non-wooden sailing vessels to be owned and registered in Atlantic Canada. Her Nova Scotia owners moved her to the London register in 1902, but did not sell her until 1908 after which she passed through the hands of three different owners, the last of them the Hudson's Bay Company, before government acquisition in April 1918. She was re-registered in the name of the Shipping Controller within a matter of weeks, but conversion on the Clyde (with another pair of eight-cylinder Vickers diesels) was not undertaken until 1919. After re-sale to Shell, the vessel was re-registered as a tanker in October 1919. Like the *Fennia*, the *Oweenee* received a fairly drastic overhaul, in this case retaining only one un-rigged mast. She also sailed for the Mediterranean, and was operating there when tardy official sanction of her new name, *Ortinashell*, caught up with her.

The last of this final triumvirate was probably the most famous, and almost certainly the only vessel that would have gone anywhere other than the scrapheap if Shell or the Shipping Controller had not stepped in. Another 1902 product of McMillan's Dumbarton yard, she was launched as the Uruguayan sail training ship *Ama Begonakoa*. She may well have been too much of a luxury for a small South American maritime power. One way or another she was laid up by 1910 when Devitt and Moore purchased her to replace the ageing *Port Jackson* in their cadet training venture and brought her back into service as the *Medway*. Less than 20 years old and restored to prime condition, she might well have sailed on well into the peacetime era. Devitt and Moore were certainly unwilling sellers (although a sale price of £41,000 will have helped ease the pain), and given that there were other, more obviously redundant, sailing ships about, it does seem a shame that she was consigned to a less glamorous future as the *Myrshell*.

The prolonged transformation of the sailing ship *Medway* into the motor tanker *Myrshell* gives an insight into the long distance nature of the Shell conversion programme. The *Medway* actually made her final departure from the UK on 12th September 1916, when she sailed from Barry Docks for Santos via St Vincent in the Cape Verde Islands. She departed Santos on 9th December of the same year for the Chilean nitrate port of Tocopilla. Between February 1917 and April 1918 she made three round trips to South Africa, and was actually lying in Capetown when the Shipping Controller acquired her on 30th April 1918. The London register book was updated to show the new owner's name on 21st May, but the ship herself departed South Africa for Colombo seven days later, still with her original Devitt and Moore crew aboard. After a two-week stay in Ceylon, she finally arrived at Hong Kong on 1st September 1918, where her mercantile crew agreement was finally terminated and her master relieved on 15th November. Conversion was completed at Hong Kong in March 1919, and she was re-registered as a motor tanker on 28th April 1919, still under the name of the Shipping Controller. She also received a pair of eight-cylinder Vickers diesels, but structural alteration was more in line with the earlier Far East conversions than the other two ships sent to the Mediterranean with the vessel emerging rigged as a three-masted schooner. Formal sale to Shell took place on 8th September 1919, but the name change, in this case to *Myrshell*, was again not authorised until December 1920, and the vessel's certificate was only amended to show the new name at Singapore on 10th April 1922.

Post-conversion careers

Only a few of Shell's sailing ship conversions were to enjoy particularly long or active careers. The *Gaper Shell*, as already noted, was lost before the conversion programme was even complete. By the summer of 1921, only months after she had finally gained her new name, the *Fionashell* was being used as a storage vessel at Piraeus, and later the same year the *Horn Shell* was consigned to a similar role in the Far East. The *Circe Shell* was reduced to a depot ship in April 1922 and was sold at Yokohama at the end of the same year. The *Myrshell* in turn was consigned to a harbour role, this time at Singapore, in 1923. Finally, in 1925, the *Fionashell* and the *Horn Shell* were both sold out of the fleet, the former to a Gibraltar-based subsidiary and the latter to the Japanese.

Four vessels thus saw out the 1920s in Shell ownership, but of these the *Myrshell* remained a depot ship, while the *Ortinashell* was restricted to service in the Red Sea. Only the *Dolphin Shell* and the *Scala Shell* were actively engaged on deep-sea service, both in the Indian Ocean and

Far East. Three vessels were sold for scrap in Japan during the Great Depression, the *Dolphin Shell* and *Scala Shell* at the end of 1931, and the *Myrshell* in April 1933. This left only the *Ortinashell*, which was sold in 1937, again as a storage hulk, to a Shell subsidiary in Egypt.

Both the *Circe Shell* and the *Horn Shell* appear to have been broken up in Japan within a few years of their sale and were deleted from 'Lloyd's Register' in 1926-7. At the outbreak of the Second World War, therefore, only the *Ortinashell* and *Fionashell* were still afloat, performing harbour storage duties at either end of the Mediterranean. The former survived to go to the breakers in 1946, but the *Fionashell* enjoyed the unusual distinction of falling prey to an Italian 'human torpedo' attack, being sunk at Gibraltar on 20th September 1941 by explosive charges undoubtedly intended for a more important target.

Shell's sailing ship conversions were presumably conceived as nothing more than a stop-gap measure. However pressing the need for tonnage might have been, war-induced inflation made the project a relatively expensive one. In the mid-1930s, Shell provided the Inland Revenue with details of the acquisition costs of most of its ships in an attempt to win tax relief for capital losses incurred on vessel disposals. These returns included the five former sailing ships disposed of between 1925 and 1931. The costs in question varied considerably. While the *Horn Shell* had cost a fairly modest £35,034 to acquire and convert, the equivalent figures for *Fionashell*, *Myrshell* and *Scala Shell* were £72,400, £76,000 and £98,000 respectively, while the *Dolphin Shell* topped the list at a hefty £135,126. There is no obvious explanation as to why the *Horn Shell* was so cheap compared to her fleet mates. The two most expensive vessels were the pair which remained in active service the longest, so it seems fair to assume that their final cost included a fair amount of maintenance and repair work, particularly in the case of the *Dolphin Shell*, whose hull was a decade older than her compatriot, and which had received a far less comprehensive initial conversion.

As a tanker, *Scala Shell* retained her clipper bow although a substantial bridge and accommodation structure was added amidships. *[World Ship Society Ltd. collection]*

Dolbadarn Castle was another baldheader, and was commanded for many years by John Baxter, who went on to take charge of the *Scala Shell*. *[John Naylon collection]*

FLEET LIST

1. GAPER SHELL   1917-1919

O.N. 98824 1,422g 1,036n
237.5 x 36.4 x 21.2 feet
Two 4-cyl. 2SCSA oil engines by J. and G. Bolinders, Stockholm; 640 BHP, 7 knots.
11.7.1891: Launched by Charles Hill and Sons, Bristol (Yard No.17) for Charles Hill and Sons, Bristol as the three-masted barque GLADYS (1,363g/1,345n).
5.9.1891: Registered at Bristol (9/1891).
8.7.1897: Sold to Shaw, Savill and Co., London.
3.7.1912: Sold to the Taltal Shipping Co. Ltd. (S.J. Eggar, manager), London.
24.7.1917: Acquired by the Anglo-Saxon Petroleum Co. Ltd., London.
30.7.1917: Registered at London (135/1917) still as a sailing vessel.
16.1.1918: Renamed GAPER SHELL.
7.5.1918: Registered at London (172/1918) following conversion at Hong Kong to a twin-screw motor tanker.
25.1.1919: Wrecked on Matamede Island, near Angoche whilst on a voyage from Singapore to Beira with a cargo of benzene and kerosene.
2.4.1919: Register closed.

2. DOLPHIN SHELL 1917-1931

O.N. 108228 2,008g 1,603g
267.0 x 40.1 x 23.5 feet
Two 4-cyl. 2SCSA oil engines by J. and G. Bolinders, Stockholm; 640 BHP, 7 knots.
18.6.1897: Launched by William Hamilton and Co., Port Glasgow (Yard No.131) for John Holman and Son, London as the three-

Dolbadarn Castle after conversion *[Photographic Services, Shell International Ltd.]*

masted barque HAYTOR (1,989g/1,860n).
1.7.1897: Registered at London (94/1897).
26.11.1898: Sold to Robert Ferguson, Dundee.
27.1.1899: Transferred to the Earnmount Sailing Ship Co. Ltd. (Robert Ferguson, manager), Dundee.
4.10.1901: Renamed EARNMOUNT.
18.10.1901: Registered at Dundee (8/1901).
10.2.1905: Sold to Robert Thomas and Co., Liverpool.
14.2.1905: Registered at Liverpool (12/1905).
3.3.1905: Renamed DOLBADARN CASTLE.

8.3.1905: Transferred to the Dolbadarn Castle Ship Co. Ltd. (Robert Thomas and Co., managers), Liverpool.
27.7.1917: Acquired by the Anglo-Saxon Petroleum Co. Ltd., London.
13.8.1917: Registered at London (143/1917) still as a sailing vessel.
16.1.1918: Renamed DOLPHIN SHELL.
22.5.1918: Re-registered at London (196/1918) after conversion at Hong Kong to a twin-screw motor tanker.
27.11.1931: Register closed on sale to Japanese ship breakers for £1,800.

3. CIRCE SHELL 1917-1922

O.N. 98320 2,810g 1,798n
296.0 x 45.6 x 25.7 feet
Two 8-cyl. 4SCSA oil engines by Vickers Ltd., Barrow-in-Furness; 1,260 BHP, 8 knots.

6.2.1892: Launched by Barclay Curle and Co. Ltd., Whiteinch (Yard No.374) for Robert Shankland and Co, Greenock as the four-masted barque CELTICBURN (2,654g/2,499n).

19.3.1892: Registered at Greenock (6/1892).

9.10.1908: Sold to Thomas Shute and Co., Liverpool.

27.10.1908: Transferred to the Ship Celticburn Co. Ltd. (Thomas Shute and Co., managers), Liverpool.

7.12.1917: Acquired by the Anglo-Saxon Petroleum Co. Ltd., London.

15.3.1918: Registered at London (64/1918) still as a sailing vessel.

8.4.1919: Renamed CIRCE SHELL and re-registered at London (122/1919) after conversion to a twin-screw motor tanker.

4.1922: Reduced to a depot ship in the Far East.

12.1922: Sold at Yokohama to the Rising Sun Petroleum Co. Ltd. for use as a storage vessel.

14.3.1923: Register closed.

1927: Deleted from 'Lloyd's Register'.

4. HORN SHELL 1919-1925

O.N. 99741 2,413g 1,507g
284.4 x 41.9 x 24.5 feet
Two 8-cyl. 4SCSA oil engines by Vickers

The *Circe Shell* retained all four of her masts after conversion to a tanker. *[J. and M. Clarkson collection]*

Ltd., Barrow-in-Furness; 1,260 BHP, 9½ knots.

23.12.1891: Launched by Workman Clark and Co. Ltd., Belfast (Yard No.89) for Sir Richard Martin and Co., Dublin as the four-masted barque HOWTH (2,244g/2,166n).

8.3.1892: Registered at Dublin (3/1892).

27.6.1904: Sold to E.A. Beazley and John Edgar, Liverpool.

8.7.1904: Registered at Liverpool (55/1904).

14.7.1910: Transferred to the Howth

Shipping Co. Ltd. (John Edgar, manager), Liverpool.

14.10.1913: Sold to Frank Windram and Co., Liverpool.

22.2.1918: Acquired by the Anglo-Saxon Petroleum Co. Ltd., London.

8.3.1918: Registered at London (55/1918) still as a sailing vessel.

12.4.1918: Renamed HORN SHELL.

24.10.1919: Registered at London (527/1919) after conversion at Hong Kong

The *Howth* could not lay any claim to speed. In 1903 and 1904, she took 201 days from San Francisco to the UK, 76 days longer than the *Californian* which left San Francisco just one day earlier. *[John Naylon collection]*

The converted sailing ships seem to have been rather camera-shy, but not *Scala Shell*, of which two further photographs have been found. *[Ian J. Farquhar collection: Ships in Focus]*

to a twin-screw motor tanker.
10.1921: Reduced to a depot ship.
17.9.1925: H.W. Malcolm, Osaka empowered to sell vessel at Yokohama for not less than 60,000 yen.
24.9.1925: Sold for £4,839 to Nippon Yusosen Kabushiki Kaisha, Tokyo for use as a storage hulk.
18.11.1925: Register closed.
1926: Sold to Kikutaro Aoyagi, Japan.
1926: Presumed broken up and deleted from 'Lloyd's Register'.

5. SCALA SHELL 1918-1931
O.N. 139002 3,585g 2,092n
330.0 x 47.0 x 27.3 feet
Two T.3-cyl. by Cooper and Craig Ltd., Dundee (16"/26½"/43" x 30"); 150 NHP, 900 IHP, 10 knots.
10.2.1902: Launched by Archibald McMillan and Sons Ltd., Dumbarton (Yard No.382) for B. Wencke Sohne, Hamburg, Germany as the four-masted barque URANIA (3,283g/3,097n).
30.1.1906: Sold to Rhederei Akt. Gesellschaft von 1896, Hamburg.
14.9.1914: Captured by the British cruiser HMS DIANA in the English Channel and sold as a prize to Speedonia Ltd. (R.D. Brailli and Co., managers), Cardiff.
4.5.1915: Registered at London (181/1915) as SPEEDONIA.
12.6.1918: Sold to Anglo-Saxon Petroleum Co. Ltd., London.
14.9.1921: Renamed SCALA SHELL.
22.3.1922: Registered at London (98/1922) after conversion to a twin-screw steam tanker.

12.1931: Sold to Japanese ship breakers for £4,500.
2.1.1932: Arrived at Osaka for demolition.
4.1.1932: Register closed.

6. FIONASHELL 1919-1925
O.N. 99952 2,444g 1,790n
284.2 x 42.1 x 24.5 feet
Two 8-cyl. 4SCSA oil engines by Vickers Ltd., Barrow-in-Furness; 1,260 BHP, 9½ knots.
11.6.1892: Launched by Workman Clark and Co. Ltd., Belfast (Yard No.93) for the Goodrich Ship Co. Ltd. (James R. Brady, manager), Belfast as the four-masted barque GOODRICH (2,243g/2,153n).
16.7.1892: Registered at Belfast (14/1892).

17.6.1895: Sold to Henry Drew, Ludlow.
21.6.1895: Register closed on sale to Raumo Nya Skeppsrederi A/B (J.W. Soderlund, manager), Raumo, Finland and re-named FENNIA
1907: Sold to Finska Rederi A/B (W.A. Soderman, manager), Helsingfors, Finland.
1911: Owner re-styled A/B Finska Skolskeppsrederiet.
1918: Acquired by the Shipping Controller (Anglo-Saxon Petroleum Co. Ltd., managers), London.
22.7.1919: Register re-opened at London (382/1919) after conversion to a twin-screw motor tanker.
8.9.1919: Acquired by the Anglo-Saxon Petroleum Co. Ltd., London.

Fionashell in the 17-month period when she sailed as *Fennia*. *[Photographic Services, Shell International Ltd.]*

14.12.1920: Permission granted to rename FIONASHELL (vessel's register altered 4.3.1921).

5.1921: Employed as a storage vessel at Piraeus.

31.7.1925: Sold to Mackintosh and Co. (Gibraltar) Ltd., Gibraltar for £8,000 for use as a storage hulk.

11.9.1925: Registered at Gibraltar (1/1925) in the name of Oil Fuel Depots (Gibraltar) Ltd., Gibraltar.

20.9.1941: Sunk in the Bay of Gibraltar by explosive charges from a piloted torpedo (Maialis) launched from the Italian submarine SCIRE.

23.5.1942: Register closed.

7. MYRSHELL 1918-1933

O.N. 129109 2,636g 1,661n
300.0 x 43.2 x 24.8 feet
Two 8-cyl. 4SCSA oil engines by Vickers Ltd., Barrow-in-Furness.

26.5.1902: Launched by Archibald McMillan and Sons Ltd., Dumbarton (Yard No 384) for Cia. Anon. de la Fragata Ama Begonakoa (Sota y Aznar), Montevideo, Uruguay as the four-masted barque AMA BEGONAKOA (2,511g/2,299n).

1906: Transferred to Compania Naviera Sota y Aznar, Montevideo.

1910: Sold to Thomas Lane Devitt, London and renamed MEDWAY.

7.7.1910: Registered at London (62/1910).

16.12.1910: Transferred to Devitt and Moore's Ocean Training Ships Ltd., London.

30.4.1918: Sold to the Shipping Controller, London.

21.5.1918: Registered at London (192/1918) with Anglo-Saxon Petroleum Co. Ltd., London as managers, still as a sailing ship.

28.4.1919: Registered at London (208/1919) after conversion at Hong Kong to a twin-screw motor tanker.

8.9.1919: Acquired by the Anglo-Saxon Petroleum Co. Ltd., London.

14.12.1920: Permission granted to rename MYRSHELL (vessel's register altered 10.4.1922).

5.1923: Reduced to a depot ship at Singapore.

4.4.1933: Register closed on sale to Japanese ship breakers for £1,500.

8. ORTINASHELL 1919-1937

O.N. 100264 2,603g 1,561n
309.0 x 42.0 x 24.6 feet
Two 8-cyl. 4SCSA oil engines by Vickers Ltd., Ipswich; 1,260 BHP, 9½ knots.

5.8.1891: Launched by Richardson Duck and Co., Stockton-on-Tees (Yard No.393) for the Oweenee Ship Co. Ltd. (F.C. Mahon, manager), Windsor, Nova Scotia as the four-masted barque OWEENEE (2,432g/2,334n).

29.9.1891: Registered at Windsor, Nova Scotia (10/1891).

11.2.1902: Registered at London (26/1902).

The beautifully-maintained *Medway*, ex-*Ama Begoñakoa*, was kept in the Australian trade by Devitt and Moore prior to the First World War. Besides accommodating upwards of 20 cadets, she could lift a deadweight cargo of 4,000 tons. *[John Naylon collection]*

After her conversion the *Medway* retained three tall masts, and had a rather primitive bridge structure added. *[Photographic Services, Shell International Ltd.]*

20.7.1908: Sold to the Thames and Mersey Shipping Co. Ltd. (William Lewis and John Herron, managers), London.

28.4.1913: Sold to the Ship Carnarvon Bay Ltd. (Samuel Roberts, manager), Liverpool.

8.5.1917: Sold to the Hudson's Bay Company, London.

4.4.1918: Sold to the Shipping Controller, London.

21.5.1918: Registered at London (193/1918) with Anglo-Saxon Petroleum Co. Ltd., London as managers, still as a sailing vessel.

8.9.1919: Acquired by the Anglo-Saxon Petroleum Co. Ltd., London.

14.10.1919: Registered at London (498/1919) after conversion to a twin-screw motor tanker.

14.12.1920: Permission granted to rename ORTINASHELL (vessel's register altered 4.3.1921).

8.12.1937: Sold to the Shell Company of Egypt Ltd., London as a storage vessel.

1946: Sold to Egyptian ship breakers.

1.11.1947: Register closed.

The *Owenee* was photographed under tow on the Avon. Although built in 1891, the same year as *Howth*, she carried the classic clipper rig of three skysails (here sent down) over single topgallants and royals. She was one of the fastest ships during the last days of sail, going from Prawle Point to Port Pirie in 66 days on her maiden passage. *[John Naylon collection]*

PUTTING THE RECORD STRAIGHT

Letters, additions, amendments and photographs relating to features in any issues of 'Record' are welcomed. Communications by e-mail are quite acceptable, but senders are asked to include their postal address. Letters may be lightly edited.

The editors would deem it a great kindness if readers submitting letters for this column would as far as possible follow our current editorial style, and in particular put ships names into upper and lower case italics and not capitals.

Umbre and *Hermes*

John Behenna's caption is correct. The salvage vessel alongside the stranded *Umbre* on page 37 of 'Record' 41 is the *Hermes* of the Swedish Bergings och Dykeri A/B 'Neptun' ('Neptun' Salvage and Diving Company). She was presumably stationed to cover the western approaches, like many salvage tugs before and since.

Hermes was built as *Meteor* in 1888 by A/B Motala Mek. Verkstad, Lindholmens Varf, Goteborg then sold to the Neptun Company in 1890 and renamed *Hermes*. She was rebuilt and lengthened in 1944 and scrapped at Goteborg in 1961.

Most of the Neptun fleet had the white band on their funnels on a sleeve of greater diameter than the funnel itself, presumably to avoid heat damage to the paint. This became a tradition and was applied to their modern motor tugs! It was spotting that detail which led me to a company history 'The Log of the Neptun Company' by A. Mattsson published in 1970.

JOHN BARTLETT, 6 Cottenham Park Road, London SW20 0RZ

On page 38 of this article the date of the second stranding of Llandaff *should have read 2nd October 1899 and not 2nd November. Thanks to Tony Smythe and Bob Todd for pointing out this error. Ed.*

Tuscan Star: origins and passenger numbers

A comment about Captain Kinghorn's wonderfully entertaining article 'A quick trip to New Zealand'. I've made a study of those two most interesting sisters, *Empire Abercorn* and *Empire Clarendon*, and all that he says about the latter's worldwide voyaging under her several names fits in with my records. I am slightly mystified, though, by his seeming reference to over 100 passengers in two classes at the time he joined her (as *Timaru Star*) at the end of 1957. He also says that 'when the immediate post-war rush of passengers diminished' the centre castle accommodation was converted to cargo space, retaining presumably sufficient (beneath the boat deck?) for the usual 12 passengers which are subsequently mentioned right up to her last homeward voyage later in 1968. The text reads as if this happened in about 1958 when *Timaru Star* was being prepared for transfer to the West Coast of North America route and renamed *California Star*. Part of such preparation was to install an additional pair of kingposts immediately forward of the bridge, apparently to cope with the extra cargo now to be loaded into the bridge-deck spaces previously occupied by second class passengers. The timing of the fitting of the kingposts is probably right regardless, because I found on the Internet

a photo of *Timaru Star* dated 1956 still without said additional kingposts.

I thought I had these two ships taped but Captain Kinghorn has cast doubt on things. All the sources I have seen to date say that *Empire Clarendon* carried 35 passengers in a single class, and that the number was reduced to the regulation 12 in 1948. I think the latter must be right, but I wonder whether Captain Kinghorn (on page 57) is giving the details of the ship as built. She might well have taken 100 or more 'inducement' passengers in austerity conditions (albeit the first class cabins were said to be 'comfortable') when voyaging to Australia/New Zealand for the Ministry of War Transport in 1945-46. Those numbers would then have been reduced on her becoming *Tuscan Star* in February 1947 to a maximum 35 in one class, to be further reduced to 12 in August 1948 when renamed *Timaru Star* for the New Zealand trade. Another clue is in the caption to the upper picture of *Tuscan Star* on page 57, which notes the large number of portholes along her bridge deck - this was where the second class mentioned by Captain Kinghorn were housed, and the openings must have been blocked off by 1949 when the lower photo as *Timaru Star* was taken, by which date the then 12 passengers would have been accommodated above bridge deck level.

Incidentally, if you tap 'Ship Tuscan Star' into Google you will find an image of *Empire Abercorn* at number 11 of the first screen. No date or place is given, but I believe it shows the ship in her original colours, black hull with thin white riband, white upper works and black funnel. She still sports her eight wartime life rafts. Because the bridge deck is painted black, no port holes are discernible, although I would assume they were there. The publisher is State Library of Victoria, so the location may well have been Melbourne.

ROBERT LANGLOIS, Feu Follet, Maisons au Compte, Vale, Guernsey GY3 5HF

I enjoyed 'Record' 41 but would add the following to Captain Kinghorn's excellent article on *Empire Clarendon*. He does her a small injustice: she did not start life as a 'mere Empire boat' (nor for that matter did *Empire Abercorn*). The design was based on the second (1937-39) and third (1943-45) series of 'R' ships built for Union-Castle, and shared the same dimensions and machinery. The principal changes were that number 3 hatch was moved forward of the bridge and wheelhouse structure (eliminating the island bridge) and that additional superstructure was built on for the 100 or so passengers, which was a requirement of the Ministry of War Transport rather than of commercial owners. Two further vessels were ordered to the design by Union-Castle, emerging in 1946 as *Riebeeck Castle* and *Rustenburg Castle*. In their case Union-Castle's Chairman Sir Vernon Thomson, who was highly placed in the Ministry of War Transport, managed to persuade the Ministry to drop the passenger requirement following VJ Day, so the Castle ships were completed as their predecessors, barring the re-arrangement of the bridge and number 3 hatch. Although the order for these ships was subsequent to the Empire order, the line of development is quite clear when the extraneous superstructure is removed.

ALAN S. MALLETT, 3 College Close, Coltishall, Norfolk

Two of the Union-Castle's reefers mentioned in Alan Mallett's letter are shown. Above, the unfortunate *Roxburgh Castle* of 1937 leaves Liverpool on 21st August 1937; she was torpedoed off the Azores on 22nd February 1943. Below, *Richmond Castle* of 1944, which survived until 1971, photographed on 31st May 1953. *[John McRoberts; Tom Rayner, both J. and M. Clarkson collection]*

Not so shabby *Imperial Star*

Sadly, Rex Cox (who wrote the otherwise excellent article on Hobart visitors in 'Record' 39) had not studied the photo of *Imperial Star* closely (page 173). If he had, and knew something about how ships worked round the Australian coast, he would have seen that she was not 'distinctly shabby' at all. There is not a speck of rust or uncleanliness on her white paint – those marks overside are undercoat applied after spot scaling as was practised all the time especially on an older ship. Patches of rust would appear under the black topside and boot-topping paint for no apparent reason, and were scaled off by lads working overside on a punt or stages. At least three undercoats were applied before the whole hull topside was painted gleaming black, ready for the long run home.

A close look at the funnel will reveal that the white funnel line is painted with red lead. My guess is that the mate and bosun decided to scale the white line completely rather than spot scale it, then do the red lead undercoats and get the white on as quickly as possible before Mr Vestey saw it! You always put at least two white undercoats over red lead before applying gloss.
CAPTAIN A.W. KINGHORN, 15 Kendal Avenue, Cullercoats, North Shields, Tyne and Wear NE30 3AQ

Blyth, bulbous bows and bronchial symptoms

Contrary to what is said in 'Blyth's Last Colliers' ('Record' 31), the three Blyth-built colliers mentioned all had bulbous bows. I was employed as a plater at the shipyard at the time these ships were built and along with others faired most of the bilge plates. Between the *Pulborough* and *Rogate*, the Blyth yard completed two (not six) dredgers, the *WD Tideway* and one for the Calcutta Harbour Authority plus two hoppers for this operator. Two hoppers, *WD Hoyle* and *WD Hilbre*, were launched but not completed and were towed away to the Verolme Dockyard at Cork. As the article stated, the keels for two more hoppers were laid but the contracts and steelworks were transferred to the Clyde.

In 'The Paint Man Cometh' by A.W. Kinghorn in 'Record' 31, there was no mention of the hazards to health these paints caused. I vividly remember one welder hanging over the ship's rail vomiting violently after working in a side tank, and this was just one occasion out of many. The symptoms were similar to those of influenza. There was even a local name for this ailment, the 'galvannies'.

I sincerely hope Captain Kinghorn's company was not responsible for supplying the paint for the Felixstowe pontoon that was built at the Blyth yard. Most of the steel for this large box-like structure came in ready painted a dull silver-grey colour which went by the trade name 'Vedette'. It was only after most of the units had been prefabricated that the paint was found to be highly toxic and its use banned. Extractor fans were supplied too late.
EDDIE CAIN, 25 Bader House, Wensleydale Terrace, Blyth, Northumberland NE24 3EY

Length or beam?

In the article 'Shell Tankers on the Mersey' in 'Record' 41 it is stated the reason the *Caurica* and the *Cardissa* never transited the Manchester Ship Canal to Ince Oil Berth was because of their beam. At that time we MSC tug men were under the impression that the reason was the bulbous bow was too large so that the overall length prohibited their presence in the canal. I must stress though that this was never officially confirmed. Perhaps other readers could throw some light on the matter?
COLIN LEONARD, 60 Halton Road, Runcorn, Cheshire WA7 5SB0

More veteran tugs

The evocative pictorial tribute to veteran British-built tugs in 'Record' 40 reminded me of the pleasure in encountering some of these old-timers in Mediterranean ports in the late 1970s and early 1980s.

Four former Alexandra Towing tugs found their way to the Italian port of Brindisi, where they were operated by Fratelli Barretta fu Comenico. They included the steam tug *Strepitoso*, ex-*Canada*, which was built by Cochrane of Selby in 1951 and engined by Charles D. Holmes of Hull. In July 1979 it was a delight to watch her from Hellenic Mediterranean Lines' *Castalia* assisting the Greek ferry into her berth at Brindisi after an overnight passage from Patras.

Strepitoso, ex-*Canada* at Brindisi, 17th July 1979. *[Peter Myers]*

Among several tugs which nudged British India's *Uganda* into her berth at Piraeus at the end of a cruise of the eastern Mediterranean in February 1982 was the splendid old steam tug *Georgios L. Matsas,* which had been built in 1946 as the *Empire Zona* by Fleming and Ferguson of Paisley for the Ministry of War Transport. She was transferred to the Admiralty in 1949 and renamed *Resolve* in 1958. The Ministry of Defence (Navy) retired her from service at Chatham in 1974 before she was sold that year to Loucas Matsas and Sons of Greece.
PETER MYERS, 69 Westbank Park, Old Meldrum, Inverurie, Aberdeenshire AB51 0DG.

J.W. Grainger has kindly pointed out that in the background of the photograph of *Dritto* on page 216 of the 'Veteran British-built Tugs' feature in 'Record' 40 appears another former London steam tug. This is one of two sisters launched by Alexander Hall and Co. Ltd., Aberdeen for British Government account and acquired before completion by W.H.J. Alexander Ltd. One contender is *San Cataldo,* shown here, which was launched as *Empire Leonard* and then quickly became *Sun XV.* She was sold to Rimorchiatori Napoletani and renamed in 1962, and was scrapped in Palermo during 1985. The other possibility is *Rania G,* intended to be *Empire Margaret* but completed as *Sun XVII.* She was acquired by the same Neapolitan owners in 1968 and broken up at Palermo in 1983. *[J. and M. Clarkson collection]*

BOSUN'S LOCKER

This issue of Record has turned out to be one of those where it has been difficult to fit everything in and where several more pages would have solved many problems. However, financial constraints do not allow us the luxury of extra pages in every issue. Consequently there are no new pictures for identification in this issue but we already have several lined up for the next issue - space permitting, of course. What we have, and are very grateful for, are plenty of notes relating to pictures in 'Records' 40 and 41. In the meantime please keep looking at the ones in back issues which remain unsolved - you may suddenly come up with answers for us.

6/40
Several readers have asked whether the lattice work apparent on this photograph of the CAM ship *Empire Spray* is indeed part of the ship's structure, or is on shore, part of a grain elevator, or another ship behind. Ian Farquhar re-examined the print, and is convinced that the structure is mounted on the ship itself.

Only one positive suggestion has been received, a very interesting one from Tony Smith. He agrees that it is an

early radar, a Type 14, from which everything detachable by spanner has been removed. The Type 14 rotated in a horizontal plane and gave a reasonable coverage for 50 miles or so when steady and mounted on a 50-foot tower on land. However, if the wind speed rose above 30 mph a mechanic and assistant had to climb the tower and rotate the scanner manually to a position in which a heavy bolt could be inserted. This prevented the scanner rotating wildly in the wind and doing itself a mischief. The manual rotating device comprised a car steering wheel to which a vertical metal rod was welded, the system being completed by two cogs and a motorcycle driving chain. It was bad enough performing this operation on land, and the difficulties of doing so at sea can be imagined. It was also difficult to obtain radar information if the wind was strong enough to cause the tower to vibrate, so the structure on *Empire Spray* may well be the remnants of an experiment which failed.

7/40
J.W. Grainger believes this ATA-type tug is *Frosty Moller* owned by Mollers Towages Ltd. of Hong Kong. She was built in 1942 by Defoe Boat and Motor Works, Bay City,

Michigan for lend-lease to the Royal Navy as *BAT 9*, although this was quickly amended to the less prosaic HMS *Destiny*. Mollers bought her in October 1948 and renamed her *Frosty Moller*, changing this to *Christine Moller* in July 1950. Mollers certainly used a white letter M on their funnels, but most photographs show the background colour as black, whilst that in 7/40 appears lighter, and possibly blue. In 1951 *Christine Moller* was sold to Dutch owners as *Oceanus*, passing to Smits in 1953 who rebuilt her as *Gele Zee*. Loucas Matsos of Piraeus bought her in 1964 and named her *Atlas*. She was last heard of as the Greek *Atlas II*.

1/41

This photograph inspired much detailed correspondence, and even our quoting the misleading information on the back of the print - which gave the name as *Aquila* - did not deter the photograph detectives amongst our readers. As we had hoped, the location proved very recognisable: the photo was taken at the Great Western Railway berth in St Peter Port Harbour, Guernsey and in the right background is the seaward side of Castle Cornet, not a headland as we supposed.

There certainly was an *Aquila* serving the Channel Islands, belonging to the Weymouth and Channel Islands Steam Packet Co. Ltd. Built in 1854 by James Henderson of Renfrew with engines by McNabb and Clarke of Greenock, she originally ran between Harwich and Antwerp for the North of Europe Steam Navigation Company. In April 1857 *Aquila* was chartered by the nascent Weymouth company who purchased her the following November, and ran her until 1889. She then passed via a London shipbroker to the Plymouth, Channel Islands and Britanny Steamship Company for service from Plymouth to the Channel Islands and St. Brieuc. Sold and renamed *Alexandra* in 1895 and *Ruby* in 1896, she was broken up at Calais in 1899. Unfortunately, this *Aquila* looked rather different from the vessel in 1/41, as it had a clipper bow and two funnels aft of the paddles.

The consensus is that 1/41 actually depicts the Weymouth and Channel Islands Company's *Brighton* of 1857. She was built by Palmer Brothers of Jarrow, and in her first year ran from Newhaven to Jersey for H.P. Maples, who was closely associated with the London and South Western Railway. She was purchased by the Weymouth company in 1858 which operated services to Jersey and Guernsey until 1889.

Jerzy Swieszkowski points out that *Brighton* can be identified from a photograph in Kevin Le Scelleur's 'Channel Islands Railway Steamers'. Both show an almost vertical bow, two thin funnels one of which is ahead and one abaft of the paddles, a distinct half-round entrance between the bow and foremast, and a diagonal waste pipe prominently entering the front of the after funnel. A third steamer on the service, *Cygnus*, was very similar in appearance to *Aquila*, having also been built for the North of Europe Steam Navigation Company. Jerzy suggests the photograph of *Brighton* was taken before 1876 when she was overhauled at the Victoria Graving Dock on the Thames and acquired a whale-backed forecastle which stretched as far back as the fore mast. *Brighton* was lost on 29th January 1887 when she struck rocks north of Guernsey in fog and sank in Little Russel Channel, all 23 passengers and 24 crew being saved.

David Hocquard reckons the steamer in the centre background, of which only the foremast and funnel are visible, belongs to the London and South Western Railway Company and is possibly their *Fannie* (654/1859).

Thanks to Alistair Deayton, Fred Hawks, Dave Hocquard, Robert Langlois, David Lodge and Jerzy Swieszkowski for the above details.

2/41

John Bartlett has worked away at this image of the Upper Pool of London, and come up with convincing identifications for the three outer steamers. He reckons that the photograph was taken from Rennie's London Bridge (which is now in Lake Havasu City, Arizona) between 1894 when Tower Bridge was completed and 1903 when the steamer *Cygnet* was lost. The steamships are, from left to right:

Ravensworth, already identified and described.

Cygnet, built in 1883 by Gourlay Brothers at Dundee for the General Steam Navigation Company, London and lengthened in 1892. *Cygnet* caught fire and sank on 29th December 1903 about 60 miles south of Vigo, whilst on a voyage from London to the Mediterranean with general cargo.

Montañes, built in 1878 by Gowan and Wilson at Berwick for M. Saenz & Co., Sevilla, Spain. She was sold in 1892 to La Betica Empresa de Nav. a Vap. also of Sevilla and was wrecked at St. Alban's Head on 3rd November 1907 whilst on passage from Spain for London with general cargo.

Ardle, built in 1888 also by Gourlay Brothers, Dundee for the North Sea Shipping Co. Ltd., Dundee. She was sold to the Ardle Steamship Co. Ltd., Dundee in 1895 and to Angus Shipping Co. Ltd. in 1904. In 1906 she was sold to Sweden and renamed *Stella* (of Helsingborg) and in 1917 *Jonkoping II* (of Stockholm). The German submarine *UC 49* torpedoed her on 24th January 1918 three miles east of Bell Rock on passage Goteborg for Hull with general cargo.

John asks if anyone can confirm the identification of *Cygnet* with a photograph. The ship with deck cranes must be a Navvy and he believes *Cygnet* is the only name in their fleet at that time with lettering compatible with that seen in the photograph.

Thanks also to George Robinson for his work on this photograph.

3/41

The double-ended paddle steamer *Gem* in this photograph also generated much interest, and there are three, very different, candidates.

The oldest of these was the *Gem* owned by the Southampton, Isle of Wight and South of England Royal Mail Steam Packet, better known as the Red Funnel Line. Built for the Isle of Wight Steam Packet Company by J. White of Cowes in 1840, she was acquired by Red Funnel in 1861. This *Gem* was based in Cowes as a tender to passenger liners in Cowes Roads and appears to have been relegated to cargo work in 1869. She was sold in 1884 and broken up in 1889.

In 1868 a wooden double-ended ferry named *Gem* was built on the banks of the River Yarra at Melbourne. Originally owned by Captains Cole and Devlin and licensed for 500 passengers, she ran from the railway terminal at Sandridge (Port Melbourne) to Williamstown until 1911. Photographs suggest that this *Gem* had a paddle box design similar to that in photo 3/41, but had two funnels.

The third candidate is the former Wallasey ferry *Gem*. Built in 1858 by Robert Napier, Govan for W.R. and E.W. Coulbourn as *Liscard*, she was iron-hulled, flush-decked and double-ended and could carry over 400 passengers. *Liscard* was intended for the New Brighton service but proved unsatisfactory and was sold in 1861 to J. and P.L. Henderson for service in the Clyde and renamed *Gem* but was then re-acquired by the Coulbourns. In July 1863 she passed to Bristol owners who used her on a ferry service across the Bristol Channel from New Passage to Sudbrook. In July 1864 the Bristol and South Wales Union Railway Company opened a branch to Sudbrook and took over the running of the ferry, placing their own vessel on the service. The redundant *Gem* was then sold to the Wallasey Local Board who had, meanwhile, taken over the Mersey ferry service to Wallasey.

On 26th November 1878 *Gem* was crossing the Mersey in thick fog when she ran into the anchored three-masted ship *Bowfell* of 1864, owned by T. and J. Brocklebank. *Bowfell's* bowsprit swept the *Gem's* deck causing the funnel to collapse on to passengers, several of whom were killed and others injured, whilst some panicked and jumped overboard. As the date on the picture matches that of this collision, it was undoubtedly taken soon afterwards. *Gem's* funnel lies on the deck, whilst the tall thin funnel belongs to the smaller vessel berthed alongside her. T.B. Maund and Martin Jenkin's book 'Mersey Ferries Volume 2 – The Wallasey Ferries' (Black Dwarf Publications, Lydney, 2003) has on page 35 a photo of the *Gem* taken from the quay showing the fallen funnel in exactly the same position and confirming that it is the result of her collision with the *Bowfell*. There is no doubt that photo 3/41 shows this vessel, the only mystery being the location, as the buildings in the background do not appear to be typical of contemporary sheds in Liverpool or Birkenhead Docks.

Gem was repaired and continued in operation until 1881 when she was sold for service in West Africa. On her delivery voyage she left Holyhead for the Brass River and had to put into St Mary's Roads, Scilly on 1st November 1881 to take on coal and repair leaks following heavy weather off Cornwall. She was run ashore for the leaks to be attended and then moored to a buoy with her starboard anchor down in St. Mary's Pool to await reasonable weather. On 21st November a west north west gale sprang up, the mooring and anchor parted and she was driven onto the rocks, broadside to the shore, to become a total loss. There is a Gibson photograph of her wreck reproduced in Richard Larn's 'Cornish Shipwrecks, Volume 3: The Isles of Scilly' (David and Charles, Newton Abbot, 1971) showing a large gap amidships where the engines, boiler, paddle wheels and superstructure have been salvaged.

We are very grateful to John Anderson, Alistair Deayton, Geoff Holmes, David Lodge, Tony Smythe, Jerzy Swieszkowski and Bob Todd for their contributions to this debate, and for the wealth of information they provided on the three vessels suggested.

4/41

Robert Langlois, Peter Myers, John Woodley and others have provided information about the *Ulimaroa*, shown aground in the River Tay. She was the penultimate ship in a series built for Huddart Parker starting with *Westralia* (2,884/1897). Each vessel was a development of its predecessor, ranging from *Zealandia* (2,771/1899) through *Wimmera* (3,022/1904), *Riverina* (4,758/1905) and *Ulimaroa* (5,777/1908) to a second *Zealandia* (6,683/1910).

Ulimaroa was launched by Gourlay Brothers at their Camperdown yard in Dundee on 20th July 1907, her name being derived from an old Maori term for Australia, which translates as 'blue and distant'. She was not completed until December, and sailed on her trials on the 2nd December, only to run aground on West Ferry beach during the afternoon. Efforts to refloat her at high water failed, and during the evening she developed a list to port. The next day the local tugs *Gilroy* and *Renown*, assisted by two trawlers, successfully refloated her at high water and towed her back to Dundee. Although no serious damage was expected because of the soft sand, it was thought prudent to inspect her hull, but as neither Dundee nor Leith had a dry dock large enough, she had to be taken to the Tyne. It was not until 4th January that she was handed over to Huddart Parker. She sailed on her delivery voyage the next day and, after calling at Durban for bunkers on 29th January, *Ulimaroa* steamed to Melbourne, arriving on 16th February. Ten days later she continued her voyage to Sydney, from where her maiden voyage to New Zealand commenced on 29th February.

Much of the above account comes from 'Huddart Parker - A Famous Australian Shipping Company, 1876-1961' by W.A. Laxon, and which was completed after the author's untimely death by H.W. Dick, I.J. Farquhar and T.S. Stevens. Volume 1 of Peter Plowman's 'Passenger Ships of Australia and New Zealand' (Conway, London, 1981) gives the date of stranding as 2nd January 1908 and suggests that no damage was done, but the date on the photograph, December 1907, contradicts this.

Gourlay Brothers over-reached themselves in tendering the very competitive price of £127,000 for *Ulimaroa* and there were some doubts about their achieving delivery. Indeed, after completing just three more ships their yard closed down in mid-1908. *Ulimaroa* lasted until 1934 when she was broken up in Japan. There is mention of her in a Ships in Focus publication due out very shortly, 'Wanganella – Awatea – Monowai. A Tasman Trio' by Andrew Bell and Murray Robinson: details appear elsewhere in this issue.

The photograph of *Ulimaroa* aground was published by Valentine and Sons, the well-known Dundee-based publisher of picture postcards.

Photo returns

'Record' relies on good quality photographs and, as we try to illustrate as many ships mentioned as possible, we rely on readers to supplement the editors' own resources. We are proud that, after using over five thousand photographs in 'Record' and many in other Ships in Focus publications, we believe that none of those lent to us has been irretrievably lost (although the Royal Mail have managed to break one lantern slide on its way to us). We advise those submitting photos or slides to clearly label them with their name, and if they do not we add details ourselves. We also ask them to be patient as, particularly with a series of articles, it can be many months before a photograph is used and returned. It is perhaps inevitable that, with the many thousands of photographs passing over our desks, we are left with the odd one or two which are unlabelled. If any readers know they lent a photograph or slide to us which has not been returned please let Roy know, with as many details as possible: again, we stress that the number of these orphans is tiny.